W9-BYL-884

Year of Jubilee

A Guidebook for Women Reinventing Their Lives

To Lineke,
Thanks for your support.
Keep growing!

Mary Heron Dyer

1999
Dandelion Seed
P R E S S
Corvallis, Oregon

Other books by author

A Ship in the Harbor

The Pastoral Associate and Lay Pastor

Year of Jubilee

A Guidebook for Women Reinventing Their Lives

Mary Heron Dyer

Foreword by
Rosemary Radford Ruether

Edited by
Vilik Rapheles

1999
Dandelion Seed
P R E S S
Corvallis, Oregon

Lindbergh, Anne Morrow. Excerpt from *Gift From the Sea*. ©1955. Reprinted by permission from Random House, Inc.

"In Impossible Darkness" by Kim Rosen from *Naked Waters*, CD and cassette on EarthSea Records ©1998.

Excerpts from Rumi, *These Branching Moments*, © 1988 by Coleman Barks, are used by permission of Copper Beech Press.

Excerpt from *Loving Kindness: The Revolutionary Art of Happiness*, © 1995 by Sharon Salzberg. Reprinted by arrangement by Shambhala Publications, Inc.

Piercy, Marge. From *The Moon Is Always Female*, ©1980 by Marge Piercy. Reprinted by permission of Alfred A Knopf Inc.

Kingsolver, Barbara. Excerpt from *The Bean Trees*, © by Barbara Kingsolver. Reprinted by permission of HarperCollins Publishers, Inc.

Tao Te Ching by Lao Tzu, A New English Version, with Foreword and Notes by Stephen Mitchell. Translation copyright ©1988 by Stephen Mitchell. Reprinted by permission of HarperCollins Publishers, Inc.

Excerpts from *The Hobbit*. ©1966 by J.R.R. Tolkien. Reprinted by permission of Houghton Mifflin Company. All rights reserved.

B. Heinrich, *A Year in the Maine Wood*, ©1994 by Bernd Heinrich. Reprinted by permission of Addison Wesley Longman.

Fulghum, Robert. Excerpt from *It Was On Fire When I Lay Down On It*. © 1989. Reprinted by permission of Random House, Inc.

Excerpts from "Burnt Norton" in *Four Quartets*, copyright ©1943 by T. S. Eliot and renewed 1971 by Esmé Valerie Eliot, reprinted by permission of Harcourt Brace & Company.

Copyright © 1999 Mary Heron Dyer

All rights reserved. No part of this book may be used or reproduced in any manner
whatsoever without the written permission of the Publisher.
Printed in the United States of America.
For information address Dandelion Seed Press, 946 NW Circle Blvd. #282, Corvallis, OR 97330.
(541)753-2819 • dandelionseed@proaxis.com

Publisher's Cataloging-in-Publication
(Provided by Quality Books, Inc.)

Dyer, Mary Heron
　　　　Year of jubilee : a guidebook for women reinventing
　　　their lives / written by Mary Heron Dyer -- 1st ed.
　　　p. cm.
　　　Includes bibliographical references.
　　　Preassigned LCCN: 98-93468
　　　ISBN. 0-9666448-7-5

　　　1. Change (Psychology) 2. Self-actualization
(Psychology) 3. Self-help techniques. 4. Women--
Psychology.　I. Title

BF637.C4D94 1999　　　　　　　　　155.2'082
　　　　　　　　　　　　　　　　　QBI98-1176

Illustrations and cover drawing by Bill Brock
Layout and design by Sue Crawford
Editing by Vilik Rapheles

Dedication

*T*his book is dedicated to Mary Dyer, my chosen namesake. Born in England, she and her husband William arrived in the Massachusetts Bay Colony around 1635. Here the Puritans preached the authority of the Bible while persecuting those who dared to believe differently. Mary, William and their children moved to Rhode Island because of this religious intolerance.

In 1652, during a trip to England, Mary joined the rapidly growing Society of Friends, the Quakers, returning to the Massachusetts Bay Colony to preach the ultimate authority of one's inner voice. Sentenced to death in 1659, reprieved on the gallows itself, she returned to Boston the following year to continue to spread the "good news" that God's voice was within every human being. In 1660 she was hanged for sedition.

Her calling was to a higher voice, her path more narrow and steep than most. May the spirit, strength and simple dignity of this woman live on in all who seek their own truth with their whole heart and mind and soul.

Table of Contents

Foreword

by Rosemary Radford Ruether

*T*he first time I met Mary Dyer her name was Mary Chandler, and she was on the rebound from cruel treatment by the Catholic church. After completing her theological studies at Mt. Angel Seminary Mary had become involved in active parish ministry at a local Catholic church, shepherding the church through a succession of interim priests while the pastor was dying of cancer, becoming virtually the pastor herself to the 2000 parishioners. Then, when a new priest was assigned to the parish, he abruptly terminated her job without a "thank you" for her faithful work.

It was the summer after that experience that I met Mary. I was a lecturer in feminist and social justice issues at Holden Village, a beautiful retreat center run by the three Lutheran synods in the hills at the north end of Lake Chelan in Washington State, where Mary was also employing her great talents in Bible study. At the same time she was struggling with her new understanding that pastoral ministry was neither possible nor worth the pain in the Catholic church, and considering transferring to what she hoped would be a friendlier environment in the Lutheran church. During that time she and I had a chance for many a conversation on the usefulness of feminists trying to do ministry and theology in the Christian churches. Mary had been wounded but was still dedicated to her vocation in pastoral ministry.

In this book I encounter Mary almost two decades later, in a new transition in her life very different from that earlier stage. Yet she still carries with her the talents, the spunk, the experience, the learnings gleaned from a history where new creativity has been all too often a precipitous response to cruel and unfair treatment by institutions that were supposed to be engaged in doing "good." Mary's book on her Jubilee Year as a gardener in training is a wonderful tribute to her own capacity for the imaginative rebound, and will be an inspiration to thousands of others caught in similar dilemmas in mid-life.

To turn adversity and injustice into an opportunity is the beginning point of this book. Who could imagine that at such a moment one can decide, not to be depressed or desperate, but to imagine yourself doing full time what you love to do anyway? As a part-time gardener who nurtures an extensive herb, fruit and vegetable garden in my urban backyard and a small adjunct garden on purloined land behind the seminary where I teach, I appreciate the choice of avocation turned vocation. Sometimes I have thought that maybe, when I retire, I will just garden....

But I probably am too much of a writer to stay long from my computer. But then, so is Mary. She had turned gardening into an opportunity for profound reflection on her life journey, and that process of reflection has become a book to resource us all. Mary distills the treasure of thirty years and more of her Biblical and theological studies, her readings in literature and poetry, her skills as a pastor turned to pastoring herself. She has learned to get herself through the low times and celebrate the good times, all with keen insight and good sense.

This handbook inviting all of us to create our own Jubilee Year is a wonderful resource; I am happy to recommend it. It is a tonic of nurturing power in the midst of an alienated world — a world that instills such fear of the free fall from paid employment that it will never let us discover that we have wings. I found great insights in it, not the least of which were some helpful hints on gardening. I discovered, for example, why my zucchini seem to grow well to four inches and then inexplicably rot at the end. What they need is fertilization from pollen of the other flower. But how do you do that, Mary? Rub the pollen at the end of the little fruit? And by the way, how do I prevent root rot on zucchini?

Rosemary Radford Ruether
Feminist theologian
Most recently the author of *Women and Redemption: A Theological History* (Fortress, 1998).

Preface

The name by which I came to call my own 50th year, and which ultimately came to be the name of this book, first occurred to me while Vilik, my partner of ten years, and I were driving the winding road from our hometown of Corvallis, Oregon to Yachats, a small town on the Oregon coast. There, in our special retreat, stretched out in front of a window facing the ocean and basking in the glow from the corner fireplace, she and I hoped to relax. I needed to unwind and recuperate from the sudden loss, just a week before, of my job at a domestic violence agency, as well as to continue to struggle with how I was now going to support myself. This crisis had also precipitated my wondering, again, what I really wanted in life. And I was discovering, when I took away the anxiety about how to pay the rent, that I really didn't have the answer to that question.

Some years before, I had gone to seminary and worked in lay ministry in the Catholic church, and bits and pieces of scripture still occasionally surfaced in my brain. On that ride to the coast I found myself remembering an idea from the book of Leviticus — an idea that was an extension, as it were, of the Sabbath, the seventh day, a day set apart in the *Old Testament* as holy, when no business was transacted, no chores were done — a time for family, food, and remembrance of God. Even slaves and animals had this day of rest.

It followed that every seventh year was a sabbatical year, when the fields would lie fallow while the people lived off the bounty of the previous years' grains. And the year after seven times seven years, the fiftieth year, was a truly special year. During this Jubilee Year people in bondage were released, lands mortgaged to others redeemed, debts forgiven. It was a wonderful time for people to rest, reassess their lives, restore their spirits.

You are to count seven weeks of years — seven times seven years, that is to say, a period of seven weeks of years, forty-nine years...You will declare this fiftieth year sacred and proclaim the liberation of all the inhabitants of the land. This is to be a jubilee for you; each of you will return to his ancestral home, each to his own clan. The fiftieth year is to be a jubilee year for you; you will not sow, you will not harvest the ungathered corn, you will not gather from the untrimmed vine. The jubilee is to be a holy thing to you, you will eat what comes from the fields…. The land will give its fruit, you will eat your fill and live in security. (Leviticus 25)[1]

My first thoughts after I lost my job had been: "How will I live?" "How can I survive?" "What can I do now to support myself?" It was so tempting to let fear of the unknown overtake me, to push myself right back into the workforce, into the same kind of frustrating job I had just left. But as I reflected on the idea of a Year of Jubilee, I decided to give myself the greatest gift of all. What I needed was a year to heal, to rejoice, to try new things. And I now had an answer to the anticipated question, "What do you do ?" I would answer, "I'm celebrating my Jubilee Year."

I returned from that trip to the coast refreshed and renewed, with a new sense of purpose. I would take this year, my Year of Jubilee, to discover my joy and follow it, trusting in the universe, as best I could, to provide for my needs.

I began in May to do yardwork for friends, little more than digging and transplanting at first. As my skills and stamina increased I began to select plants myself, put in pathways, build fences and even a treehouse. The summer passed blissfully as I actually did what I loved and got paid for it. In the fall I decided to go back to school to get a one-year horticultural certificate from the local community college. With work-study, student loans and some maintenance and landscaping, I could manage. For the school year of September 1996 through June of 1997 I was hip-deep in soil science, plant biology, arboriculture, plant propagation, integrated pest management, tree and plant ID — to name a few.

But that winter also brought divorce, depression and sickness. My husband and I had been separated for over ten years, a separation that involved my leaving the family home and "coming out." To provide as much continuity and stability as we could, Harry and I had remained legally husband and wife, and had never stopped being friends. But now our kids were grown. A daughter, Ann, lived in Eugene and was planning her wedding; a son, David, was in college in Portland studying English literature. Our youngest daughter, Margaret, who lived with her dad, was just finishing her senior year in high school. The time seemed right for Harry and me to take the final step of divorce.

But I was unprepared for what that step would bring with it. Having remained friends with my "ex" over the years, I was taken aback by the intensity of the divorce proceedings, stunned over "unfinished business," overwhelmed by my feelings.

What I had thought was going to be a fairly easy process became at times acrimonious as we struggled to figure out how to share the still co-owned house and Harry's retirement benefits. Harry had always been in many ways my best friend, but at times I was not sure we would even end up on civil terms with each other.

December found me in deep depression, tired, irritable and hard to be around, a situation that did not seem remedied by the Prozac I now took every day. My partner, who lived next door, wisely took the month "off," going to visit friends in California, leaving me to muddle through on my own. Then, after Harry and I reached an agreement that left both of us slightly, but equally, unhappy, I caught a cold in January which turned into severe bronchitis and held me firmly in its grip until March. On top of that I received a questionable mammogram in February that needed further evaluation. And all these physical problems came about just at the time I was losing health insurance because of the divorce.

But spring finally came, the sun shone again, and gardens beckoned. A year to the day of my Jubilee Year I began a part-time job at a retail nursery, which had been one of my goals. My landscaping business continued to grow. Referrals came to me of their own accord, alleviating my need to seek customers. I had more work than I could handle, each job providing its own challenges and chances to hone my skills. It gave me such satisfaction to learn how to earn my living with my hands and my heart, to meet the unique needs of being self-employed, of not having a boss to placate. And a new and more spacious home attested to both my growing sense of self-worth and my new-found financial independence.

I realized that my Year of Jubilee had been an apprenticeship — not to gardening in and of itself, but to my own spirit. The working with my hands, not my head, the sheer digging in the ground, the physical exertion of a "hands on" job, had become my daily spiritual practice. I had learned to work with the life breath of the earth, to track the path of the sun, to feel the seasons through the tips of my fingers. And I had learned the seasons of my own life. I had discovered the difference between struggling and trying hard, between forcing and flowing. I had witnessed the universe mysteriously yet constantly provide the tiniest seedling, the greatest tree, the daily sustenance each needed to flourish. And, slowly and hesitantly at first, I had learned to trust that the same wisdom which told the plant when to pull into itself, when to stretch out its rootlets into new soil, was a wisdom I shared. I learned — each day — that each day was enough. Each day I would be given all I needed. Not so much to make a living, as to create a life.

Through it all I journaled, searching out my life purpose, examining what freed me, what still held me captive in old patterns of thought. From time to time I shared entries with friends, or at Unity of Corvallis. In January of my Jubilee Year excerpts from my journal were published in *Unity Magazine*, and many readers let me know how that entry touched a chord in their own lives. This response convinced me to go back into my journal entries and look at the central themes. Perhaps my struggles and insights could be organized into a self-help journal for other women — a Year of Jubilee self-help book for anyone willing to risk changing her life.

Introduction to your Jubilee Year

*A*nne Morrow Lindbergh's *Gift From the Sea* is a perennial favorite of many women. In it she shares reflections which came to birth during a week at the seaside. One in particular strikes my fancy:

> *Perhaps middle age is, or should be, a period of shedding shells; the shell of ambition, the shell of material possessions, the shell of the ego. Perhaps one can shed in this stage in life as one sheds in beach living; one's pride, one's false ambitions, one's mask, one's armor. Was that armor not put on to protect one from the competitive world? If one ceases to compete, does one need it? Perhaps one can at last in middle age, if not earlier, be completely oneself. And what a liberation that would be!*[2]

Some of us may be older, some younger, than the middle age about which Lindbergh writes so insightfully. Yet our task is still the same — to be completely oneself. Indeed, what a liberation that would be!

This book is structured to give you an opportunity to become more completely yourself. The organization is not chronological, so you will not be reading the story of my year "in order" (although I have added the dates of each journal entry, for those interested). Rather, I have organized the chapters around the central issues that emerged during my own Jubilee Year, and have chosen entries from my journal that illustrated those ideas.

Twelve chapters take you through the year. There is a sequence to the chapters, but they are not carved in stone. While I was arranging the ideas for the chapters, they frequently changed places with each other as I played with them. So, it is possible to jump in anywhere, to a chapter that suits your needs.

I have also found that this Year of Jubilee has no end. The themes in it are part and parcel of human life, and it is virtually impossible to really be "done" with one theme and then master another. Hopefully you will enter each topic at a higher and higher level of consciousness as you walk down your life's path, but seeing the "sights" from different angles at different times of our lives just makes the journey all the more interesting.

In each chapter there are four weeks' readings, each week ending with a journal assignment, a meditation, an exercise and an artwork assignment for a Year of Jubilee collage (one of the things I did during my own Jubilee Year). I fully believe that if you go through this book, either by yourself or, more powerfully, with a group of other women, your life will change in dramatic and exciting ways. How could it not? You are being given an opportunity to look at your heart and follow your joy. Is there anything more important? Is there any doubt that the universe will support you in your quest? So let us begin....

ENDNOTES

1. *The Jerusalem Bible.* NY: Doubleday and Co., 1966. *(*Note: All scriptural quotations will be taken from this source).*

2. Lindbergh, Anne Morrow. *Gift from the Sea.* NY: Random House, Inc., 1955.

Acknowledgments

*T*his book has been such a team effort. Yes, I wrote the journal and arranged the chapters, but without the support of three people this book would have stayed in the realm of spiral-bound copies reproduced at a local copying place.

I wish first to thank Sue Crawford, the initial person I told I was turning my journal into a self-help book for women. Her immediate words were, "Let me help you." She proceeded to give of her prodigious talent in layout and design, including dealing with the printer, to make this a truly well-put-together work.

Second, my thanks to Bill Brock. He took my idea for a book cover and turned it into something beyond my wildest dreams. He also took my childish scrawls and turned them into wonderful graphics for each week, adding a dimension I could only imagine.

Lastly, Vilik Rapheles. Partner, friend, you have taught me more about living than anything else. Truly this book would not have come about without you. Your eye for detail and ability to hold to the "big picture," and your continued belief in this project and in me, even when I had my moments of doubt, have made this work a real "gem," each little piece enduring your close scrutiny and inspired editing.

Beyond the book, my life during and after my Year of Jubilee has been filled with the love and support of many people. As a member of the board of Unity Church of Corvallis, I met every other week with John Luna, Gene Gipe, Valerie Vike, Kay Fischer, John Wolcott, Greg Watson, Dick Kutsch and Bill Brock as we steered the church through its year without a minister, until Neusom and Cathy Holmes came along to take the helm. To these special people, as well as more Unity friends than I can name, I owe the sense of spiritual community that allowed me to write this book.

Then, of course, there are my landscaping clients, who gave me not only the pleasure of working on their land but the paychecks that brought food to my own table. Cheryl and Gene Gipe, Sue Crawford, Nancy Dimmick-Spain, Greg and Lynn

Dimmick, Ted and Sandy Wadman, John and Jody Gaylord, Cheryl McLean, Debra Livingston, Pam Mathews, Joanne Malkin, Fran Harper, Leonard and Luma Litman, Sharon Sherlock and Nancy Weber, you have truly given me a chance to earn my keep "by the (profuse) sweat of my brow."

"The Carolines", the old Victorian apartment house where I lived while I wrote this book, was another source of community. Mina and Mina, my special landlords, even had us tenants over for brunch on occasion. So many people have lived there during my stay; some special names are Till, Penny, Laura, Kate, Kelly, Barb, Sherri and Karen. Although I'm no longer at The Carolines I'm now only next door. On the other side of my house I have the good fortune to have Dale Green and Wanita Miller and their two special children, Christopher and Maggie, as neighbors.

For the pieces written at the ocean, and even more for the time just to "be," I am grateful to Carl and Deb Ramsay and their cozy "peek of the ocean" condo in Newport, as well as to the healing powers of the ocean view and fireplace at the SeaVue in Yachats.

There were friends at the agency against domestic violence who supported me before and after I lost my job, some of whom still put their wonderful talents and skills into making this world a safer place for women and children. Thank you, Teresa Guajardo, Mary Zelinka, Jannie Wahl, Janet Vandecoevering, Rhiannon Ashe, Sue Gifford, Christine "ToWanda" Rhea, GayLynn Pack.

Greg Paulson, my teacher of horticulture at Linn-Benton Community College, opened my eyes to the intricacy and balance of the natural world which my classmates, Susan Fleming, Barb Bolden, Beth Deimling, Chris Reichert, Wendy Campbell, Gloria O'Brien and Linda Brewer, shared with me. And Michael Thompson helped me put it all into practice.

For showing me the possibilities of openness and intimacy I thank spiritual teacher and workshop leader Kim Rosen. For reading my manuscript and giving me faith as well as encouraging words I thank Jody Stevenson and Rosemary Radford Ruether. For taking me further on the spiritual journey I thank everyone in Unity's Continuing Education Program, with special thanks to Don Jennings and Jim Gaither. For being a longtime friend and support I thank Joyce Baxter.

And finally, of course, my family, beginning with my children, Ann, David and Margaret, each different yet whole and complete in their own special ways. My mother, Esther Anthea Moisson, who gave me my special love for animals; Vilik's mother, Ophelia "Pat" Conroy, who fortunately passed along the editing gene. Bill and Jean, and Peggy and George, who give me a sense of roots. My ex-husband and always friend, Harry, and my new son-in-law, Kirk.

I could go on and on, but I guess I have to stop somewhere. Listing all these wonderful people makes me think of community support as Barbara Kingsolver describes it in *The Bean Trees*,[1] using, of course, my favorite horticultural imagery:

> *It's like this...There's a whole invisible system, for helping out the plant that you'd never guess was there...The wisteria vines on their own would just barely get by...but put them together with rhizobia and they make miracles.*

INTRODUCTION ENDNOTES

1.   Kingsolver, Barbara. *The Bean Trees*. Harper and Row: NY, 1988.

In Impossible Darkness

Do you know how
the caterpillar
turns?

Do you remember
what happens
inside a cocoon?

You liquefy.

There in the thick black
of your self-spun womb,
void as the moon before waxing,

you melt

(As Christ did
for three days
in the tomb)

congealing
in impossible darkness
the sheer inevitability
of wings.

— Kim Rosen

I

Charting a New Course

*The real voyage of discovery consists, not in seeking new landscape,
but in having new eyes.*

— Marcel Proust

Introduction

*U*ntil a few years ago I was on a course that seemed to be taking me where I thought I wanted to go in my life. Retirement, savings — I had plans. Apparently I hadn't yet heard the joke that begins, "Do you know what makes God laugh?" In April of 1996 I was fired from my job without notice, my only warning being the upset stomach, sore shoulders, and general feeling of pressure and discomfort that had become an integral part of my work day. It was then that I experienced firsthand the truth behind that joke. "What makes God laugh?" Why, "Telling God your plans," of course.

Not everyone is lucky enough to get fired when they really need to, as I was. Sometimes we keep hanging on because an uncertain or unclear future seems less threatening than a certain present, no matter now predictable or possibly even toxic the present may be. Yet there is a part in each of us, a part that tells us the truth, that lets us know when we have stopped growing, when life is no longer joyous.

This first chapter of *Year of Jubilee* is designed to help you examine your life as it is. Is it meaningful? Is it joyous? Is it creative and life-affirming? If you can answer a resounding "yes" to all these questions, this book is not for you. Go to a movie or treat yourself to a novel. But if you hesitate, if you are unsure, and certainly if you would answer "no" to any of these questions, take a risk, turn the page, and get to work on your new future. Only you can take that first step.

NOTES

WEEK ONE

Losing the way

Sometimes it takes a sudden jolt
to set you on a new path

Woman overboard!

April 25, 1996

This morning I was sitting at my desk in a domestic violence agency, dealing with an always unfinished list of crises resulting from too little time and money, too many women and children in life-or-death situations. The work overload left us all, at best, frantic — at worst, in tears. Recruiting, training and supervising volunteers for the hotline, shelter and as group leaders was the easy part of my job; making sure the hotline was staffed 24 hours a day by volunteers with their own busy lives was my daily burden. "Sorry Mary, I can't do this shift — I'm pregnant"; "my mother died"; "I'm too busy." Tick-tock, tick-tock, tick-tock...the minutes of the office clock inched agonizingly toward that next uncovered shift.

On my own time, away from a job that kept me always aware of a sense of lack, I had begun to explore ideas like *Energy flows where attention goes*, and *The universe conspires to give us what we want*. Part of me believed these intriguing new concepts and wanted to try them, but another part held on tightly to a job that no longer gave me joy. I thought I needed the salary, the accumulated vacation time, and, of course, the proposed 4% pay increase the board was thinking about... maybe. But I had also been able, finally, to arrange my schedule so I had one day a week to take part in a Master Gardeners' class. Gardening was my passion, and I daydreamed about my life ten years in the future — gardening, spiritual study and practice, perhaps a small private counseling practice. But those dreams were on the distant horizon...so distant I could barely make it out.

I had been examining my beliefs about money, trying to break through the Protestant work ethic engraved on me by two depression-era parents. But I still kept thinking in pennies, in dollars, on a linear time/space continuum. If I brought in $1,400-1,700 a month, my credit card debt would be paid off by June of 1997 and my student loans by 1999 at the latest. These figures became mantras, constantly in the background of my thinking. I promised myself I would follow my heart's desire …someday…when the bills were paid and I had enough savings.

But today my carefully calculated plan exploded. I was fired.

I had written a letter directly to the board of directors of my agency, explaining the crisis mode we had been operating under this last year and presenting some "do-able" solutions to the major problems. But the board and director decided my attempt to question the agency at all was "insubordination." The axe fell at 2:00 p.m. this afternoon.

I had an hour to clean out my desk, take down my pictures of Israel, the 2′x3′ collage I had made for my fiftieth birthday a few months before, pack away my favorite coffee cup, say my goodbyes. My last act before turning in my keys — the keys that had opened the door to my job as a worker in the domestic violence movement and to a central part of my identity over the last few years — was to pick up my plants. The door slammed as I left, a sound that resounded through my soul.

But as I put my plants in the car, I saw, through my tears, that the last one I loaded, a prayer plant, had a beautiful surprise. I had been too busy to notice it was in full bloom for the first time, its beautiful, broad-leafed black and green leaves covered with tiny white flowers. And as I drove home, still in shock, nothing left of my life as a domestic violence worker but the remnants in the back of my car, I couldn't help but notice the lilacs nodding in the spring breeze and the wisteria cascading over porches to form arbors of soft lavender or crisp white. The dogwoods were blossoming, despite not having jobs, and the mayberries looked about to pop open with multitudes of tiny pink flowers with no help from a savings account. All this abundance moved me deeply, and left me thinking.

Perhaps, like the prayer plant, it is time for me to unexpectedly bloom.

EXERCISES

• JOURNAL

The famous 13th-century poet and mystic, Rumi, wrote in his poem, *Become the Sky*[1]:

Take an axe to the prison wall.
Escape,
Walk out like someone suddenly born into color.

Are there things or people in your life that no longer bring you joy? Write about them, along with why you hold on to them. Are there things you might not even be aware of because it would be too threatening? What prison walls still keep you in?

[Go out and buy a pretty book with blank pages. Use this to do the journal entry above and jot down any other thoughts that may come up for you during the week.]

• INNER WORK

In prayer or meditation (using language comfortable to you) contemplate the serenity prayer.

God (Goddess, Higher Power) grant me the serenity
to accept the things I cannot change,
the courage to change the things I can change,
and the wisdom to know the difference.

[This will be a way to help you get out of your logical mind as well as your "little self." The ideas in this book are based on the concept that we are all part of something bigger than our limited physical and material view of ourselves. You may call it intuition, higher self, God or Goddess, or only your wishes. Part of your experience this year will be learning to quiet yourself through some form of prayer or meditation and get in touch with that "still, small voice" within you that speaks your deeper truth.]

• EXERCISE

As you go about your week and engage in your usual activities, notice when your "joy quotient" is high — and when it dips.

[This will be something concrete, in the real world, to reinforce the lesson for the week.]

• YEAR OF JUBILEE COLLAGE

Get a piece of poster board, white or colored. This will be your Year of Jubilee collage. You can mount it in an open frame if you want. Look at the emptiness of the space and be receptive to this new beginning, a year of possibilities as yet undiscovered.

[This will be a way for you to "keep track" of your journey during the year and will become a beautiful reminder to you of this rite of passage.]

WEEK TWO

Luck is partially just being prepared

Opportunity will knock, so start getting ready

Luck is being prepared for opportunity when it comes
April 27, 1996

Morning: The little rats of money worries woke me early this morning, gnawing at my innards. It's just been a couple of days since I lost my job and I can't apply for unemployment until a "waiting week" has elapsed. I don't even know if I'll get it anyway, since I was fired. And yesterday my credit union turned down my loan request.

As each "rat" chewed its way into my consciousness, I tried to shoo it away. But Friday, when I'm supposed to know something about my unemployment, seemed an eternity away. Time to get out of the house!

I drove toward the east, where hints of coral slowly tinted the sky behind the still-dark hills. As I began to sing the harmony to my "Alleluia" tape, I looked up to see the stark outline of a red-tailed hawk perched on a telephone pole, its feathers etched on the dawning sky. Just as the sun peeked over the horizon it flew off its perch, hovered for a moment, then dived, landing on its unsuspecting prey.

It knows better than I, it seems, that the sun will come up, as it always has, that the newborn light will reveal the bounty of the freshly-plowed field. All it has to do is wait, trust, and be ready.

This day, like the vigilant and calmly expectant hawk, I will dare to believe.

Evening: I went to the Unity board meeting after supper, despite my anxiety. It was an important one; several of us from the board and four from the congregation were meeting as a search committee to go over applications for the position of minister. During the meeting I told everyone I had just lost my job. I also told them I needed to find work fairly quickly. Before I could even finish Gene said, "Cheryl hurt her back and can't do any gardening. We'd love to have some help. When can you start?"

Sue was next. "I have a lot of yard work I can't get to, and I've been wanting to build a small pond. And I need to tear out the rotted plastic under the weeds on the slope above my house and put in some plants to hold the soil. Oh...and then there's the rock wall I've been wanting my husband to build. Can you come up and take a look at my property tomorrow?"

The universe was right there, open-handed, meeting me just where I needed to be met, responding to my act of faith through the kindness of others (and their unfinished projects!).

EXERCISES

• JOURNAL

Write in your journal a list of your assets, skills and what you see as your positive qualities.

• INNER WORK

In prayer or meditation, allow yourself to fully realize and "own" the qualities you've listed in your journal.

• EXERCISE

The paradigm below has been popular in psychology for years. It shows four areas of self-awareness: I. What everyone knows about you, common knowledge. II. What you alone know about yourself. III. What others know about you that you might not. And the enigmatic, IV. What is not yet known by anyone about you, including yourself.

Fill in what you can in your journal. (Later, you'll have the opportunity to fill in the blanks.)

JOHARI'S WINDOW

I. Everyone knows...	III. Others only know...
II. I only know...	IV. No one knows...

• YEAR OF JUBILEE COLLAGE

Find or draw something that represents your spirit or essence, and put it in the center of your Year of Jubilee collage.

NOTES

WEEK THREE

Choosing passion

If you find what you love to do,
it won't feel like work

Treehouse
July 9, 1996

What a glorious week this has been. Not only have I been building a tree-house, I've been getting paid to do it.

It was just a month ago that my landscaping client, Cheryl, and I started plotting this treehouse in top secret meetings. It was to be a birthday surprise for her eight-year-old daughter, Catie, and I would build it while the family was away on vacation in Colorado.

My job all month, until the treehouse project, was working in the front yard, digging up the soil and laying down weed barrier and sand in preparation for an aggregate stone pathway to the front door. But when lunchtime came I took my sack lunch and sat under a lovely old apple tree in the back yard. When I looked up into the branches it seemed to me the tree was just crying out for a treehouse. Soon, I promised....

This imaginary treehouse took form in my mind; the first thought to wake me in the morning and the last thought to put me to sleep at night was of the beautiful treehouse being birthed in my imagination. Finally, Cheryl and family left on vacation. I had exactly one week to take this treehouse out of my mind and, with wood and nails and sweat, turn it into a surprise birthday present that even Catie's father didn't know about.

The day before they left I was at the lumberyard at eight a.m., the only woman in a world of men — male clerks, homeowners and do-it-yourselfers, lining up three deep in front of each harassed clerk. But I held my own. I added lags, bought my very own Stanley 25' tape measure, rejected one slightly warped 2 x 4 tight knot cedar for another straighter one. Back in Cheryl's garage I got my work center set up: saw, miter box, bolts, lags, washers, monkey wrench, Swanson Speed Square, 1/4" drill, with 3/8" and 1/2" bits, sharpened pencil.

The next morning I had the 7' x 7' frame built. Then I got help putting it up in the tree from my daughter and her dad. Would the frame fit? Would the whole thing work in reality as it had in my head? The three of us carried the three-sided, open frame out to the tree. The first attempt didn't work at all, so we rotated it 90 degrees. All right! Now I could handle attaching the fourth side on my own.

The next days flew by, establishing a rhythm. The temperature was averaging 103 degrees so I got to work by seven in the morning, hammer in hand, and worked until I couldn't stand another minute in the heat. Then it was home for a bath and nap, after which Vilik and I found an air-conditioned eatery and movie — any movie — just as long as it afforded a couple hours of coolness.

The floor went in easily, although each piece had to be cut to order. I was building this treehouse without any nails in the tree. Three branches came up through the floor and I had to work around them. The balance was tricky at times; I got quite good at hanging onto the treehouse with one hand for extra support while I hammered with the other. (I didn't find out until after they returned that the stepladder was convertible to an extension ladder.)

Now the week is coming to an end; the treehouse is almost complete. The ladder to the treehouse entrance is 14 feet tall, 8 feet from the ground before it goes through the floor of the treehouse, its top extending far into the canopy of the tree. The safety railing looks really spiffy. The treehouse even has a secret side panel that can be swung open so a parent can place a small child inside without going up the ladder. A window, complete with window box, opens out to the lawn. I can hardly wait until Catie sees it.

It's been a long time since I enjoyed something as much as creating this magical, leafy-green hideaway in the heart of the beautiful old apple tree. And to think — I got paid for it!

EXERCISES

• JOURNAL

List in your journal things you've done or dreamed of doing that make you feel passionate or alive. What do you love about them? Is there a common thread?

• INNER WORK

In prayer or meditation, ask to be open to feel your passion. If it seems you can't find your love, open in a prayerful way to have it revealed to you. If you are already open, experience the passion to its fullest.

• EXERCISE

Do something you love this week for at least an hour, and let yourself experience your feelings about it.

• YEAR OF JUBILEE COLLAGE

Put on your board a representation of something you love.

NOTES

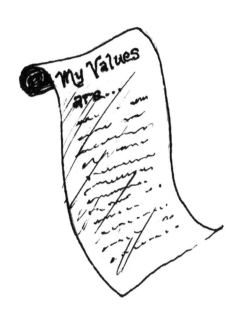

WEEK FOUR

What really matters

What are your highest values,
and are you living them?

"Soul Purpose"
June 23, 1996

As I was tidying up my apartment yesterday, I ran across some notes from a workshop I attended last winter. Jody Stevenson, the facilitator and author of *Soul Purpose*, gave an exercise in which we wrote down, in order of importance, eight organizing principles of our lives. Then, working with a partner, we challenged each other to explain them, get rid of them, or reorder their priority until we were satisfied they represented our highest and deepest sense of self. My eight were:

1.	*Gratitude*	5.	*Integrity*
2.	*Joy*	6.	*Peace*
3.	*Power*	7.	*Creativity*
4.	*Abundance*	8.	*Security*

It was exciting to find them again, now, almost two months into my Jubilee Year. It intrigued me that I had listed security last. On my "bad" days I can feel it trying to push to the top of the list, shouldering aside joy and abundance. How will school be this fall? Am I making a good career choice? Can my body continue to take the daily physical stress inherent in landscaping? But I push it back down to where it belongs on my list, so I can reclaim the most important one for me: gratitude.

Gratitude attunes me to my place in the universe and aligns me with my Source. Every morning as I wake up and each night as I go to sleep, I am grateful for this wonderful gift called life.

Integrity has always been a close second for me — to know the truth, to take a personal risk to speak the truth. *Integrity*, in fact, was what got me fired. What kind of a shadow life is it, if we are less than true to our own inner voice?

Joy is what enlivens me, allows me to feel the "juice" of life. It is what lets me know that I am, indeed, alive in this bodily form, connected to my spirit, to my soul, to my senses of pleasure and pain.

Peace is that overwhelming sense that, in the end as well as in the present moment, all is well. As Jesus said to his disciples at the Last Supper before the events of Good Friday, "Peace I bequeath to you, my own peace I give you, a peace the world cannot give, this is my gift to you." (*John* 14:27). The external circumstances are just that – circumstances. They have no more to do with my sense of being connected to a larger source than the ebb and flow of the ocean takes away its vastness or its depth.

Power allows me to live in the world on my own terms, to act on my integrity. It isn't about domination or "power over," but of letting me be a moral agent in my own life, in the world, being aware of my own importance to the universe.

Creativity is the expression of my soul on the physical plane. It is divine play, the uniqueness of this "self" expressing. "When the dancer becomes the dance, the singer the song...," when we are actually able to lose ourselves in our creativity, to be "in the flow," it may be that we are closest to our own divinity.

Abundance is knowing, not just believing, that there really is enough and that "enough" does not come at the expense of others. If indeed we have the power to create what we want from the "ethers," as it were, and not just eke it out from what already exists, then abundance has to do with my alignment with the Source and my understanding of the laws of creation.

Security follows from all the other principles. Yes, I like my "creature comforts," but I am working to understand where they come from and how they come to me, and that my security is grounded in my relationship to Source rather than the material world.

The principles I have chosen express my true self, my lifetime values. On any path I take, my course is clearly set when these eight guiding principles lead the way.

EXERCISES

• JOURNAL

Think about significant life experiences, "peak" moments, and ask yourself why they were so meaningful. What personal values emerge as you look at what matters to you? Write down your own organizing principles in order of importance. Are they being reflected in your life right now?

• INNER WORK

In prayer or meditation, ask to have your deepest values revealed to you.

• EXERCISE

Hang up your list of organizing principles in some obvious place (e.g. refrigerator, mirror). Think about how your activities right now reflect them, about how you live them out (and how you don't).

• YEAR OF JUBILEE COLLAGE

Post the list on your board.

CHAPTER ONE ENDNOTES

1. Rumi. *These Branching Moments*. Copper Beech Press: NY, 1988.

2. Stevenson, Jody. *Soul Purpose: Rediscover Your Creative Genius and Become the Champion of Your Life*. Source Communications & Publishing: Portland, OR: 1995.

NOTES

II

Gambling on Life

The universe will reward you for taking risks on its behalf.
—Shakti Gawain

Introduction

*T*he voyage has begun. The near shore has faded into the sunset — the far horizon is not yet visible. But there is no going back to the way it was; the point of no return has already been reached. It brings to mind a parable of Jesus in the *New Testament*:

> *The kingdom of heaven is like treasure hidden in a field which someone has found; [s]he hides it again, goes off happy, sells everything [s]he owns and buys the field. Again the kingdom of heaven is like a merchant looking for fine pearls; when [s]he finds one of great value [s]he goes and sells everything [s]he owns and buys it.*
>
> *(Matthew 13:44-46)*

Both the farmer and merchant have found something so valuable that they are willing to risk all they have, all they are, in the hope of possessing something they cannot live without. This journey toward one's own treasure is not for the cowardly or the weak of heart. It will take everything you have, and challenge you to go further than you ever imagined. But that's all right, isn't it? It's time.

There is a warning addressed to "fence-sitters" in the last book of the Bible, the Apocalypse. Messengers of God were sent to each of the seven towns of Asia Minor in the first century to preach the message of salvation to these far-flung little cities, now covered in sand. What the angel spoke to Laodicea can serve as a reminder of the importance of our own journey:

> *I know your works; you are neither cold nor hot. Would that you were cold or hot! So, because you are lukewarm, and neither cold nor hot, I will spew you out of my mouth...I counsel you to buy from me gold refined by fire, that you may be rich .... Behold, I stand at the door and knock; if any one hears my voice and opens the door, I will come to her and eat with her and she with me ....*
>
> *(Revelation 3:15-18:20)*

Life is profligate. Life takes risks. Life gambles all it has on itself. This chapter deals with risk-taking, inviting you to roll the dice, to sell all that you now perceive as valuable, to buy the field, to obtain that pearl of great price. It costs everything you have, but once you have seen it there will be no question in your mind that it is worth it. So open your door now. Your future is knocking.

WEEK ONE

There's lots of everything!

You live in an abundant universe

The bounty of seeds
January 17, 1997

It's already begun. Seed catalogs are stuffed into my mailbox every day. Ferry-Moss even sweetened their offer with a free packet of verbena, "Florist Mixed Colors," with these tantalizing words under a bright picture of brightly colored verbena:

> *Annual, Old-fashioned favorite. Clusters of dainty,*
> *fragrant blossoms with a long blooming season.*
> *Showy in shades of deep violet, lavender, red, pink,*
> *white, cream. Laughs at heat and drought.*

In this small package, weighing less than an ounce, are over 150 seeds (yes, I counted them), each with the potential to become a plant covered with a living bouquet of flowers. The seeds are brown dry rods, rustling quietly when I separate them into piles of ten with the tip of my pen. To the naked eye they look dead. But seeds aren't dead at all. They have stored energy; they respire; they even give off heat. There have been documentations of seeds of an aquatic lotus plant germinating after more than 1,000 years, of Arctic tundra lupine seeds that had been frozen an estimated 10,000 years coming to life. Their dormancy can last a few short days or 10,000 years, longer than the recorded history of the human race.

Something in those seeds will not be stopped — the life force is too power-ful. One day something happens to wake up the slumbering cells: the right temper-ature; just the right amount of moisture; abrasion of the seed coat through grinding of rock particles in the soil. They break open, send out baby roots called radicles, take hold of the soil, draw in its moisture and push tiny green plumules out of the soil into the life-giving sun.

I feel like one of those tiny seeds. I'm storing energy, building knowledge, feeling the seed coat being forced open by my own new life — gardens, landscapes, writing, bereavement counseling — and soon that little sprout of green will break apart the clodded earth and claim the sun as its inheritance. And I too, like the promise on the verbena package, setting my own roots deep, will learn to "laugh at heat and drought." For my spirit is programmed just as deeply and inevitably as the DNA in the little seed hidden deep in the Arctic tundra, and my destiny is just as cer-tain.

The bursting of blossoms
March 12, 1997

Just a little bit ago, I put aside the paper I was writing and took a walk in the beautiful pre-dusk light. I was struck by all the trees in blossom — cherry, dogwood, apple, hawthorn. I stopped under one particularly lovely tree to look up into the canopy covered with delicate pink blossoms, its first leaves still spring green and almost too small to be seen.

What an amazing act of faith that tree performs every spring, putting its win-ter-stored energy into producing blossoms before it unfurls its first small leaves to begin anew the task of taking the sun's power and turning it into food through the magic of photosynthesis.

And believe me, it is not niggardly. It puts all it has into the wonderfully prof-ligate display of promise, not holding back. Each branch, each stem, holds a handful of flowers, offering them to the spring.

Some trees are more "sensible," getting their leaves in line, in working order, before diverting energy into blossoms. But somehow these leafless trees, these floral risk-takers, have more to teach me. They show me that it is all right to trust in the abundance of the universe, to put forth everything I have in the act of living joy-ously.

EXERCISE

• JOURNAL

Write down any fears of lack of abundance that may come up this week. Where in your life is your belief in limitation especially strong?

• INNER WORK

In prayer or meditation, ask to be shown (through feeling, thought and experience) that the universe is rich in bounty.

• EXERCISE

Read something that talks about the unlimitedness of the universe.

• YEAR OF JUBILEE COLLAGE

Find one saying that most perfectly sums up the abundance of the universe for you and put it on your collage.

NOTES

WEEK TWO

Seeing with new eyes

All that you need is already waiting

Daily bread
September 14, 1996

What a summer I have had! I drank two gallons of water a day as I labored under the noonday sun, learning to operate a gas-powered post hole digger, paving a walk, building a fence, designing and building a tree house, learning to tell time by the movement of the sun in the trees rather than a watch on my wrist.

But now it's already fall, more days than not too cold or wet to work, winter looming just around the corner. Some days I actually have to wait for the sun to defrost the ground before I can dig, my work made especially awkward by the thick gloves I have to wear to protect my hands from frostbite. Yes, my needs were provided for this summer. But what will happen to me now that the sun — and my work — are waning?

It reminds me of the story in Exodus, when the Jews, homeless, their only possessions what they carried on their backs, without the flocks of sheep and goats that had been their livelihood, wandered the desert for forty years. Yet God assured them that their needs would be provided for every day:

Behold, I will rain bread from heaven for you; and the people shall go out and gather a day's portion every day, that I may prove them, whether they

will walk in my law or not. On the sixth day, when they prepare what
they bring in, it will be twice as much as they gather daily.

(Exodus 16:4-5)

Dew as fine as hoarfrost appeared on the ground every morning, and each day the people arose to gather and eat it:

Morning by morning they gathered it, each as much as they could; but
when the sun grew hot, it melted.

(Exodus 16:21)

Each day any remaining manna melted, and the Israelites had nothing but faith to sustain them until the following morning.

I, like those long-ago people, have been cared for all summer, my income just enough to meet my needs. Now, as I suspect they did also, I am struggling with my fear of whether there will be "manna" tomorrow.

I mulled this story over today, while I drove around and checked the sides of the road for weeds to "bag" for an assignment from my integrated pest management class. I managed to spot dandelion, Scotch broom, thistle, field horsetail, everlasting peavine, wild carrot, aster and chicory. Later this evening, while taking a walk, I discovered sorrel, field penny cress, bittersweet nightshade, Mayweed chamomile, field bindweed, creeping buttercup, lambs quarters, catchweed bedstraw, hairy vetch, red-stemmed filaree, field violet and poison oak.

Tonight I have spread out my collection of at least twenty plants, some resting on the couch between newspapers and pressed down with books, others on the floor being mounted, still others, as-yet-to-be-identified, stuck under the couch.

What amazes me isn't that I was able to find them so quickly with my "new" eyes, which see plants differently now, but that they were there all along, just waiting for me to pay attention to them. They're literally everywhere I look. I've been walking past them, walking on them and through them all my life with hardly a glance. Now I see their intricate beauty, their infinite variety, their sheer abundance. It humbles me, reminding me that all I need are the eyes of faith to see the abundance that has already and is forever surrounding me wherever I go, just waiting patiently for me to reach out and claim it as my inheritance.

And only when we are no longer afraid
do we begin to live in every experience,
painful or joyous;
to live in gratitude for every moment,
to live abundantly.

–Dorothy Parker

EXERCISES

• JOURNAL

Write about one area of your life where there is abundance you have not been able to see. What looks like a patch of "weeds" but is really a beautiful plant?

• INNER WORK

Pray or meditate on the idea: "See God in everything." Look for the bounty in everything this week.

• EXERCISE

Take a walk and observe the plants growing on the earth, cultivated and uncultivated. Enjoy them!

• YEAR OF JUBILEE COLLAGE

Find a plant or dried flower that represents abundance. Mount it.

NOTES

WEEK THREE

Trusting God's timing

Your destiny is good, and it's coming your way

Every day it gets a little closer
Part I
March 13, 1997

I've made it through my first winter of "down-time" in the landscaping business, and my year of horticulture school is coming to an end. The next step seems to be working part-time at a retail nursery. Part of my desire is to continue to learn, but part is also to have at least some steady and stable income. I think I need that. Last summer my landscaping jobs were "grace" — but what's going to happen this summer?

I applied to the largest local nursery months ago. My grades in my horticulture classes are excellent, and I have a friend who knows the owner — I was sure I was a shoo-in. Thinking the job was in my pocket has kept me from panicking. But today I learned I didn't get it. All they need are full-time workers, and I can't work full-time and have a landscaping business. I visualized, I believed, I had my plan for the spring and summer all constructed in my head. Now it's not happening the way I thought it would, and I'm feeling like a failure.

As I tried to find the "light at the end of the tunnel," I remembered two sparrow hawks I often see on the way to school. Hawks are solitary creatures as a rule, except when they pair off in spring to mate and raise their young. Well, spring is here. But these two hawks, sitting on telephone wires with a pole between them, haven't quite made up their minds about each other. Yet the writing is on the wall; it just needs a little time to develop. Soon they will come together and create a family.

Every morning as I drive by I smile at them, raising a hand in blessing, secure in my knowledge of their destiny as mates well before they've figured it out for themselves. I'd like to bring that same sense of trust to my own life this week. I guess my destiny isn't going to be at Garland's and it's hard letting go, especially when I can't quite see around that telephone pole in my own life to what's waiting on the other side.

But I do feel the presence of my own destiny. The inevitability of life, the same power that inexorably draws those two hawks together, is bringing me and my destiny closer and closer.

Every day it gets a little closer
Part II
March 17, 1997

This morning I saw the hawks again. They were sitting about a foot apart on a phone line, paired up for hunting, facing opposite directions so their sharp eyes covered all the ground beneath their razor-sharp talons. Their fate as mates seems as clear now in their own eyes as it has been all along in mine; soon they'll be building a nest.

On the home front, with me and my own fate, I can't seem to turn around without bumping into another landscaping referral. Sunday, at church, I met the sister of a client; she wants me to redo her front yard. My Sulphur Springs couple wants me to come to their house this week to discuss the details of their project. I have so many jobs lined up for the summer, I think I can support myself on landscaping alone. I still want to work at a nursery part-time — not only for for security, but to learn new skills, expand my horizons, and learn more about available plant materials. But my needs are clearly being taken care of, and time will reveal more to me — in its own season.

Year of Jubilee end
April 25, 1997

I write this at the end of my first day working at a retail nursery. It has not escaped my notice that this is also the official end of my Year of Jubilee, a year to the day since I was fired from my social service job. My work t-shirt, as yet unstained by soil or sulfur water, is bright blue, the nursery's name emblazoned across my chest. One of the old-timers took me under her wing, pointing out the locations of the sun-loving annuals, shade-loving annuals, hardy perennials and tender perennials in the large open shelter. Flower names tripped on my tongue: white licorice, bachelor's button, lamium, snapdragon, alyssum, verbena, calendula, lobelia, zinnia.

Then, with my ears already buzzing, it was on to the shade area, the shrub yard, the two tree areas, ground cover, perennials, water plants, vines, retail green-house, three working greenhouses. I wrote as fast as I could, jotting down names of plants as they attracted my eye. Every time I got a short break I wandered around, practicing where things were, trying to avoid any customers with questions in their eyes.

The day flew by as fast as the little puffs of clouds pushed by the coastal wind across the deep blue spring sky. Soon it was quitting time, my shirt no longer clean but having an honest smell of peat and soil, my shoes squeaky wet from the after-noon watering. As I climbed into my truck I felt satisfied, full, glad that I had spent my one-year anniversary here.

On the way home I found myself driving by the domestic violence shelter where I used to work. But I passed on, happy in the knowledge that my way is no longer there. Somehow, today, on this beautiful spring day full of hope, my destiny and I embraced.

EXERCISES

• JOURNAL

Fantasize your ideal destiny and write about it.

• INNER WORK

In *Anatomy of the Spirit*, Carolyn Myss[1] says that we live with the myth that once we say "yes" to God, everything will be perfect immediately. In prayer or meditation, accept that your perfect outcome is already yours, while also surrendering to divine timing.

• EXERCISE

Act "as if." Act this week with a sense that your destiny is coming.

• YEAR OF JUBILEE COLLAGE

Find a picture that represents trust (e.g., a young animal or child) and post it on your board.

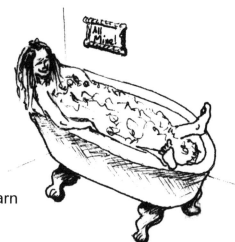

WEEK FOUR

The leap of faith

Don't look a gift horse in the mouth;
give it a bale of hay and lead it to the barn

Goodbye to thunder mugs!
August 21, 1996

Yesterday, I heard the apartment underneath mine is going to be vacant again. Without wasting a minute, I called the landlord and told her I'd take it.

This old, two-story Victorian was subdivided years ago into oddly configured apartments. The one I live in now is on the second floor, where bed, chair, desk and bookshelves fill to overflowing the cramped sitting/bedroom, and the kitchen's so small I had to take out the stove to fit in a tiny table. A two-burner hotplate serves for everyday; a toaster oven emerges for special occasions. Did I mention I don't have my own bathroom? There's a communal bathroom down the hall, shared with two other women, but, since one or the other always seems to be soaking when I most need to use it, I sometimes resort to the "thunder mug" in the closet. But even more than a bathroom I miss a porch — a place to put my plants, sit out on and "just be."

Yet I've stayed here for 5 years. It's partly because of the low rent...and partly inertia. But most of all, it's because of who I think I am and how much I think I'm worth.

About a year ago, the apartment below mine opened up — two rooms with its own bathroom resplendent with claw-footed tub, and a small private porch. But I procrastinated. Moving seemed too much trouble, the rent was higher, and besides, I was waiting for a cheap apartment to come available down the street. While I hemmed and hawed, a new tenant moved in downstairs, and the "cheap" apartment never materialized.

But now I'm ready. I want to cook on a real stove, and turn on more than one appliance at a time without having the fuse blow. And I want to hang baskets of flowers, impatiens and fuchsias and white licorice, on my porch. True, the rent is more, and I don't have a guaranteed income — I'm a beginning landscaper on unemployment, and winter is coming. But pinching pennies isn't worth it anymore, not when it also pinches my spirit.

This apartment I'm living in has been the beginning of my independence, the first place I've lived since being completely self-supporting. But it's time to take another leap. Downstairs. After I move, I'll be able to luxuriate in that deep, claw-footed tub any time I like. And I'll finally get to retire the "thunder mug" for good. Maybe I should have it bronzed, like my first pair of baby shoes. It might look good with flowers planted in it...

EXERCISES

• JOURNAL

Is there something about which you've been saying "I'm just not ready yet?" Write about why you don't think you're ready.

• INNER WORK

Fantasize what it would look like, feel like, to have the thing you wrote about. In prayer or meditation, allow yourself to be ready.

• EXERCISE

Look for opportunities to say "yes" this week to things that stretch you a little.

• YEAR OF JUBILEE COLLAGE

Draw or find something that represents taking a leap.

CHAPTER TWO ENDNOTES

1.   Myss, Carolyn. *Anatomy of the Spirit: The Seven stages of Power and Healing.* Harmony Books: NY, 1996.

NOTES

III

Self-Limiting Thought

Argue for your limits, and sure enough they're yours.
—Richard Bach

Introduction

*T*his past summer I had occasion to go to Nevada twice, a journey that took me through pine forest and high desert, as well as open range where cattle foraged. The road wasn't an interstate; no fences separated cars and livestock. But the highway department had found a simple way to attempt (with some success, I might add, since I never saw a dead cow on the road) to keep cattle off the high-speed road. Cattle guards.

Now, the interesting thing about these cattle guards was that they weren't even real. The real ones are built like slats over an open space; cattle shy away from them because their hooves get caught. What I saw on the way to Nevada, however, was simply white paint, painted onto the surface of the road in the pattern of cattle guards. The cattle had learned their lessons so well they mistook these now two-dimensional shadows of menace for the real thing.

These "trompe d'oeil" cattle guards intrigued me, and I found myself reflecting on how the cattle's response to this false image was parallel to ways I have limited myself. At many points in my life I took for real something which was simply my own fear, projected in front of my own feet and barring my way. I was also reminded of one occasion when I actually did step out and challenge the fear of what seemed to loom before me.

A few years ago I gave in to my optometrist's advice — time for bifocals. But when I got the new glasses, with their funny line right through the center, they didn't help my vision at all. Quite the contrary. I had to retrain myself to lift my head up a little for near vision, and when I took my first walk in bifocals the ground in front of me seemed to be falling away — it felt as if I were stepping off the sidewalk into a chasm.

For days, between aspirin for the headaches, I seriously contemplated going back to the no-longer-effective, single-lens prescription. Fortunately, I toughed it out. My brain was actually retraining my eyes to see differently, to override the message that the ground was opening up in front of my feet. Within a week I was outside again, walking surely, swiftly and certainly. I had overcome the sense of imbalance and falling, and now, miraculously, I was able to drive and read with the same pair of glasses.

If I had believed my senses, believed what I thought I saw, I would have kept myself from something that actually improved my life. In how many other ways do my own personal "cattle guards," many of them no longer even real, keep me from exploring the full range of my world? How do I need to retrain my brain, my spirit, my soul — to challenge my perceptions and replace them with beliefs that allow me to step out without fear of falling off the face of the earth?

Hopefully the selection of readings in this chapter will allow you, also, to look at the beliefs you still have about your own limitations, to challenge them, and to overcome them. After all, what we think we see is not necessarily what is real, as I learned with my bifocals. That "cattle guard" in front of you may be nothing but a chimera, a ghost from your past, with no more power to hold you back than a painting on the highway. No more power, that is, than that which you give it.

WEEK ONE

Negative self-talk

Thoughts are things —
are yours tripping you up?

The limits of adventure
June 7, 1996

One of my all-too-rare treats is a trip to the public library. This week I checked out the Oregon journals of David Douglas[1], a famous nineteenth century British horticulturist who explored the Pacific Northwest. Douglas, born in Scotland in 1799, worked for the Horticultural Society of London, a group particularly interested in plants growing in other parts of the world. In 1825 they sent him to America to explore the northwest corner of the United States, then a largely unexplored territory being fought over by the British, Americans, French-Canadians and Native American tribes. His journal is a wonderful mishmash of botany, adventure, geography, history and anthropology. My favorite entry is his account of an Indian sweat lodge:

> *Early in the morning left the fort for the purpose of visiting an extensive plain seven miles below on the same side of the river. Passed several Indian steaming huts or vapor baths; a small hole is dug about one foot deep, in which hot stones are placed and water thrown on them so as to produce steam; the bather then goes in naked and remains until well steamed; he immediately plunges into some pool or river, which is chosen so as not to be far distant. They are formed of sticks, mud, and turfs, with a small hole for means of entering. They are most frequently used when the natives come from their hunting parties, after the fatigues*

of war, and also before they go on any expedition which requires bodily
exertion. My curiosity was not so strong as to regale myself with a bath.

It tickles my funny bone to picture this "adventurer "— a man who traveled dozens of miles a day on foot, slept in the open under a frequently wet blanket, ate salmon, sturgeon and an occasional bird or hare, all caught by himself — yet who did not have enough "curiosity" to enter a "steaming hut." Actually, I expect it wasn't lack of curiosity that kept him away. I have something in common with Douglas, in that regard; saunas are outside my own "comfort zone" as well.

This entry of his leads me to reflect on the real nature of adventure. David Douglas certainly qualified as an explorer of the outer world. In fact, the Douglas-fir we are so familiar with is so named because he brought specimens back to England. And he died the death of an adventurer at only thirty-five when he was gored to death by a wild bull.

I, too, am an explorer. No, I don't climb mountains or portage a canoe up the Willamette or hunt my own food (unless wild dandelions and miner's lettuce count). But I do push into new frontiers of personal and spiritual growth.

And yet David Douglas and I have both been stopped dead in our tracks by something as seemingly innocuous as a sweat lodge, each of us choosing to stay on this side of that little door which opens, for those who dare, to new experience. I expect the infected knee that laid Douglas up for months in the wilderness would have healed much more rapidly had he treated it to the healing "vapors" of the "steaming hut." But he couldn't cross that threshold. It teaches me that true adventurers can't just go with our strengths, our talents, our interests, but must be open to being unsure, being uncomfortable, being on the edge.

Well, it's getting late and I pulled a muscle gardening today. I'll bet a sauna would feel good, but I won't be having one. Like Douglas, I still haven't been able to get over seeing myself as someone who doesn't take saunas.

I can't make it
November 24, 1996

I worked for a short time today, but there was little to do in the yard, still flooded from our record rainfall, where I was gardening. It was even too wet to edge the lawn, so I just weeded. The rain has kept me from working much at all lately, and I'm worried about money.

On the way home I went by the drugstore to pick up my Prozac prescription. I started Prozac a few weeks ago for a winter depression made worse by the divorce proceedings. The doctor gave me the first two weeks' supply in samples, but I've used them up; today I was to get my first prescription filled. But when I got to the drugstore and was handed the bill, I was unprepared for the expense. I had been told my cost would be $10 a month but the bill today, even after coverage by insurance, was $49.

I'd had a cold, wet, frustrating morning. The pharmacy had confused my prescription with someone else's, and kept me waiting 20 minutes. And then I got a bill I didn't have the money to pay. I was already feeling shame — about taking Prozac in the first place, about having people I didn't know find out — and now I didn't even have the money to buy it. My shame turned into anger, and I just lost it. I looked at the new price, said "Forget it!" and stomped out of the store.

Back home I ranted and raved about drug companies and HMOs , threatening to go off the medication and " tough it out alone." With no steady income and so little money I feel powerless, trapped and full of rage. I feel like a failure, and right now I don't see myself as being able to make it as landscaper. I just feel like giving up.

Crawlers
December 1, 1996

As I left for school last week, the woman in the apartment next to me called out her window to ask me how things were going. "Fine," I replied, perfunctorily. "How are you?"

"Left foot, right foot, " she replied. In retrospect, her answer was more true for me than my social lie.

All I feel able to do right now is put one foot in front of the other, slowly, methodically, trudgingly. It's hard to see the future; it's hard to keep moving at all. I'm tired, really, really tired. All I want to do is hole up, sleep in, read detective novels and watch TV, isolating myself from everyone. I find myself letting my homework slide and going to bed early.

The weather's been cold, damp and rainy, making gardening seem an unendurable chore all too easily postponed. I did manage to work six hours this weekend, raking leaves, trimming, weeding and pruning, but I had to push myself to do even that.

I've been so down on myself this past week, criticizing myself, my character, my choices, my perceived failures — the failure to follow through, to carve out a better place financially, to feel more stable and secure emotionally. My own negative judgments are harsher than any outsider's could be, because sometimes I mistake these internal voices for my own true self.

Tomorrow I'll be giving the meditation and message at church. I'm calling it "Crawlers and Reluctant Flyers,"* a title I got from my class in integrated pest management. It's a description of those familiar garden pests, aphids. They do have wings but rarely use them, preferring their rose leaf to the mystery of flight. Today, I'm definitely a crawler, unable or unwilling to use my own wings — doubtful, just like the aphids, I even have any.

* See Introduction to Chapter 12 for further explanation (p. 225).

EXERCISE

• JOURNAL

1) Complete the following phrases ten times:

"But I always..."

"But I never..."

2) What are some of the messages you learned about yourself from your parents? Which of them are no longer true? Which of them do you still tell yourself?

• INNER WORK

"Sit with" your fears of inadequacy, of failure. Are they holding you back or making you more joyful and alive? Meditate on this short poem:

> *Living is*
> *A thing you do*
> *now or never —*
> *Which are you?*
> — Piet Hein, *Grooks*[2]

• EXERCISE

Watch your self-talk in the moment. What are you telling yourself about yourself?

• YEAR OF JUBILEE COLLAGE

Find a picture or item that represents something you are afraid of or think you can't do well and put it on the board.

NOTES

WEEK TWO

Boxing in the world

What blinders do you wear when you
look at the world?

Arborvitae
March 26, 1996

On Monday I finished planting a row of arborvitae (Latin for "tree of life") as
a privacy screen on the property line between my clients and their neighbors.

Back when I was first considering this particular job and thinking about what
might be the perfect plant for the site, arborvitae naturally came up — it's a popular
hedge/screen choice. But it's also overused and often allowed to grow too big, and I
had developed an aversion to it. In fact, for years I had been telling myself how much
I disliked arborvitae.

I tried hard to find another tree/shrub that would fit the needs of the space,
but I kept coming up short. There was nothing left to do but acquiesce to the precept
we're taught in horticulture — that we cannot let our landscaping be dictated by our
own personal favorite plants. And, by derivation, I suppose that also applies to our
least favorite ones. Finally, I made my decision. In this particular space, arborvitae
would be the best option.

I found myself warming up to arborvitae more and more as I went to the
nursery and selected the five healthiest plants. Back at the site, I arranged and planted them in their pre-dug holes, watered and surrounded them with bark mulch —
and then stood back and surveyed the results with unexpected pride.

Now I enjoy their compact, sharply pyramidal forms, their vertical, fan-shaped, scale-like clusters of leaves, their neat and defining symmetry against the afternoon sun, their dark green evergreen color.

They serve as a living reminder about prejudgments that still litter my path — about food, people, ideas, preferences, beliefs. It's so easy to let our past not just prepare us for the future, but dictate it, driven by outworn, no longer useful or true "facts." This beautiful, living, growing, newly-planted hedge of these "trees of life," new to my appreciation, will serve as a reminder that life is for the present.

"I'd rather be in Philadelphia..."
August 28, 1996

The radiologist stood up to greet Vilik and me as we entered his office this morning, x-rays of my breasts eerily lighting the otherwise dark room. There was a mass in my left breast, he told us. He thought it was probably benign, and advised me to wait six months, then have another mammogram. Vilik asked about having a biopsy immediately, and I shot back, "Fine, if they use your breast!" The truth is, any medical procedure unnerves me, and the thought of lying on the operating table and having a long hollow needle stuck in my breast is terrifying.

I've always had trouble going to doctors. I hate being touched by medical people. Maybe it's because my mother was a nurse and was always treating me for something as a child, I don't know. The doctor today was kind enough, and seemed competent. But, still, I am almost as uncomfortable dealing with the medical system and relating to doctors as I am scared about the lump. I'm doing better than I would have ten years ago, though, when I wouldn't go to a doctor at all. At least I had the mammogram, and I didn't run screaming out of the office this morning.

I truly believe I'm going to live to be a feisty, fully alive old woman. If I do have breast cancer, I may need to deal a lot more with the medical system to help make that come true. I'm reminded of the old W.C. Field's joke. When confronted with the idea of death, Fields replied, "On the whole, I'd rather be in Philadelphia." (Philadelphia was a city he detested; he said they rolled up the sidewalks at 8:00 p.m.) If my choices are death or the medical system, I'm with Fields. "On the whole, I'd rather see a doctor."

EXERCISE

• JOURNAL

Complete the following phrases ten times:

"I hate ..."

"I'm afraid of ..."

Write them in your journal.

• INNER WORK

Take one long-cherished belief about the world and consider how it has limited you. In prayer or meditation, open to the possibility that your belief is only that — a belief. Ask to see the truth.

• EXERCISE

This week, as you interact with people and situations, watch the labeling going on in your own thinking. Consciously allow yourself to see past the labels.

• YEAR OF JUBILEE COLLAGE

Put up a picture of something in the world that really bothers you. Over it, put something which, for you, represents the Christ light.

NOTES

WEEK THREE

Thinking in new ways

You can challenge thoughts that hold you back
and replace them

Paper bag
October 3, 1996

It's my second week of school in a one-year horticultural program at the local community college. I have eight hours of lab every week, which may very well be the sum total of all the labs I had during the 12 years it took me to get masters degrees in English literature, scripture and theology, and counseling.

Today I had my plant science lab. We had to make our own slides of cork, onion, tomato, pepper, potato and eloides (a protozoan found in pond water). But when I tried to zero in on the cell wall of an onion, I felt all thumbs — Gulliver in the land of the Lilliputians. A thin film of anxious sweat broke out across my brow as parrot voices began their chatter in my head. "Can I do this at all?" "What if I can't?" "Why am I such a klutz?" "How do I know I'm doing it right?" And, of course, the clincher, "I was never good at science anyway." But it wasn't until I started to wonder if I needed to breathe into a paper bag to control my hyperventilating that I realized something had to change. And maybe that something was me.

Could I take charge of my experience and create a new one, an experience not driven by my bad memories of science? I tentatively tried injecting a new thought. "I can do this." Okay, that helped. How about: "I'm smart and motivated." "I can ask for help when I need it." "I don't have to be at the top of the class." I was breathing easier, relaxing. Maybe it was time to throw in a new clincher. "I like science now..." Hmm. Could I put a little more juice into it? "I *like* science *now*!"

I just kept repeating those messages over and over, working with a lab partner, asking for help, redoing a couple of slides. And by golly, I actually saw the cell sap coursing through the leaf and a little protozoan that looked a lot like a fast slug with a pointy head darting around the petri dish chasing an invisible "lunch" — a microscopic game of cat and mouse.

So I did it — a bit awkwardly, maybe not the "star" of the class — but I finished the lab assignment ten whole seconds before the end of lab. And I'll keep on doing it, hour by hour, slide by slide.

"Baby steps, baby steps"
June 18, 1996

What About Bob?, one of the funniest movies I ever saw, portrays a counseling relationship gone awry. Bill Murray stars as an extremely agoraphobic patient who fixes on Richard Dreyfuss, a successful psychiatrist, as his only hope of recovery. Murray's fear of the outer world confines him to his apartment, where he relies on home delivery for groceries and a goldfish for company. When he finally confronts his fear enough to show up at the psychiatrist's office, it just happens to be the day before Dreyfuss is to begin a month-long vacation with his family.

Murray, however, cannot wait until the end of the month, or even the end of the day, for his therapy to continue. So he tricks the doctor's receptionist into revealing where the doctor and his family are vacationing, closes up his apartment and puts the goldfish in a mason jar of water tied around his neck. He forces himself to go to the bus station, buy a ticket, board the bus and go to the doctor's retreat. Each step of the way he mumbles to himself, "Baby steps, baby steps," a mantra the doctor had left him with at the end of their first session. Each "baby step" takes him that much closer to leading a normal life, with the final scene in the movie showing him marrying the doctor's daughter.

That image of that terrified, yet doggedly determined client came to mind when I forced myself to make my first phone call to a prospective landscaping client, also a total stranger. I must admit I was immensely relieved to get her answering machine, but it was good practice for a real live person next time. "Baby steps, baby steps."

Quantum stumble

August 12, 1996

Today was a low-energy day for me. I got to work by 7 a.m. and began transplanting a cherry tree, then went on to finish cleaning up a slope where I hoped to lay a path, taking wheelbarrows filled with rocks to dump on a pile in the woods. I still seem to have my Puritanical inner clock by which I measure my daily achievement; 5 hours means breaking even on monthly bills, 6 hours measures up to my former pay, and at 7 hours I give myself a bonus. But I hit the wall early today; work just seemed tedious and flat. I kept saying to myself, "Six hours a day times five days a week times fifty-two weeks a year times ten years until retirement — I can't do it!"

Then I began to realize I don't have to do it, at least that way. I can charge more per hour and work fewer hours. I can look for good-paying, enjoyable, part-time counseling jobs with flexible hours. I can create my new world any way I consciously choose to shape it. I just have to keep letting the energy flow through me, and allow myself to unfold my wings. Maybe it's only "quantum stumbles" right now, but one day it won't matter how many rocks are on the path — I'll soar right over them in a quantum leap.

EXERCISE

• JOURNAL

Go back to weeks one and two. Rewrite your phrases with a more "open" attitude.

• INNER WORK

Pick one area where you've been "stuck." In fantasy imagine a different outcome and "talk yourself through it."

• EXERCISE

Challenge your negative self-talk. Talk to yourself like a good friend. Pat yourself on the back — literally!

• YEAR OF JUBILEE COLLAGE

Write an affirmation that confirms your specialness in language that is meaningful to you. Hang it on your collage.

WEEK FOUR

It's never too late!

Unless you're dead, you can change

You can too teach an old dog new tricks!
June 11, 1996

The first time I used a computer was several years ago at work. I was terrified. The younger women at the office seemed able to jump right in, tossing around esoteric words like "modem," "bytes," "CD-ROM" and "interface." As for me, I finally got to the point where I could at least use the computer like a typewriter, begging other office staff to take the "hard copy" (another new word!) and rearrange it so I could run it off for the newsletter.

After those helpful staff members left to go back to school, I was more on my own. Gradually I learned one or two new tricks a week — columns, bulletins, saving to another drive (after, of course, I figured out what a "drive" was) and simple graphics. It seemed, however, that each little bit I learned opened up even more I didn't know.

When I lost my job I also lost access to the computer, along with the computer expertise that went with it. I was left with my home computer, so old and outdated I considered donating it to the "catapult toss" of old computers at our town's annual fair. Finally, I unplugged my old friend and donated it to the Salvation Army, unsure if even they could use it, yet without the heart to throw it away.

Now I had no computer at all. But a new one would cost over $1,000, not counting a color printer which I also wanted.

I waffled several more weeks before I tilted towards the "new world." I had been saving $100 bills — now I had a short stack of nine. I knew that my new life had to have a good computer in it, so I finally made the call to a computer friend: "Steve? It's Mary. I'm ready to take the plunge."

After we discussed how much I could pay, I shared my main concern. "My biggest fear is that I'll get a computer beyond my competence to manage, but I'll probably need more than word processing if I go back to school."

We talked for awhile, then I took another leap of faith. "And what about being 'on-line'? (another new word!) How does that work?"

Soon we were discussing modems, phone lines, e-mail, database systems, cost. And I committed. "Yes, I want a modem."

I'm not exactly charging full steam into the twenty-first century, but I'm walking as fast as I can. I hope Steve never moves out of town. But, hey...there's always e-mail!

The new world is here
August 3, 1996

It finally happened. Before eight this morning, Steve arrived with my computer. Fortunately for me he had already programmed it; we just had to fit it into its new home, put the printer disk information on the computer's hard drive, and plug it in.

Questions tumbled out of my mouth. "How do I access WordPerfect?" "How do I get my modem set up?" "Who do I call if something goes wrong?" (the last one being the most crucial!).

I even understood some of the answers.

I still need a printer cable and some new formatted disks and paper ... but it's here! Along with its promise of new skills and adventures. Steve even programmed in some computer games for me. If all else fails, I can play Crazy Eights with a computer-generated dog.

maryherondyer@proaxis.com
August 9, 1996

What a strange day! From sod webworm in class to hard drives at home, from *bacillus thuringiensis* and gooseneck lysimachia to modem, from hands thrust into the earth to fingers flying through cyberspace. I'm on the net! My head is still spinning with new terms and new skills to learn, just like my new gardening and landscaping career, but I'm on the way!

The computer installer arrived this afternoon, just after I'd finished washing layers of clay soil off myself. I was waiting for a service truck, like the ones that belong to cable TV or the gas company, but a young man pulled up in a convertible and just carried in a slim black briefcase. It's hard for me to "grok" this new world. I managed to be slightly helpful, getting the new phone line plugged in, rearranging the desk top. I even managed a couple of what I thought were intelligent questions. But mostly I just sat there and nodded my head as he worked his computer magic. I finally told him I wasn't an oral learner. I needed to see it in black and white and work through it myself.

I'm lying in bed now, looking across the room at this blank-faced, resting piece of high-tech equipment. It's hard to believe all I have to do is cross the room, turn it on and I can either check the local movie listings, contact someone in India or Germany about the origin of Dutch elm disease, or download on a printer with 32,000 color combinations.

I guess the trick, as always, is to keep my sense of balance, to keep my feet firmly on the ground and familiarize myself with the expanded knowledge this new tool will offer me. So I'm signing off for now. Over and out.

maryherondyer@proaxis.com

EXERCISE

• JOURNAL

What represents "the new world" to you? How is it out of your grasp? Write about it.

• INNER WORK

In prayer and meditation, open to your own marvelous competency.

• EXERCISE

Pick something you haven't thought you could do. Take that first "baby step"!

• YEAR OF JUBILEE COLLAGE

Think about a time when, after some struggle, you finally mastered a particular skill. Put something on your board which represents that.

CHAPTER THREE ENDNOTES

1. Douglas, David. *The Oregon Journals of David Douglas and his Travels and Adventures among the Traders and Indians in the Columbia, Willamette and Snake River Regions During the Years 1825, 1826 and 1827.* (Publisher, date unknown).

2. Hein, Piet. *Grooks.* Doubleday and Co.: NY, 1966.

IV

Self-Nurture and Support

I have found God in myself and I loved her fiercely.

—Ntosake Shange

Introduction

*A*s I was growing up I had two major myths about myself that I later took into adulthood: the myth of the "Lone Ranger" and the myth of the "Spartan Boy." The first allowed me to live out my childhood with some sense of adventure and purpose — I envisioned myself as the loner who did incredible feats of good, then disappeared without thanks. There were many like him in those long-ago days — Superman (another favorite), Zorro, Paladin — all of them feeding my fantasies of saving the world, one crisis at a time. I still vividly remember the time, when I was five or six, my mother took me to meet "Superman" in person in some large department store. I was already a tomboy, strong for my age. When I finally got up to him, towering over me in his red and blue tights, I looked up at him and said, "Can I pick you up?" He declined (it would probably have damaged his image) but I still know in my heart of hearts that I could have done it!

My other mythical hero, the Spartan boy, supposedly lived millennia ago as part of a warrior culture in the small city-state of Sparta, in the Greek isles. As the story goes, he had stolen two baby foxes, wrapped them up inside his tunic and taken them to school. While he was denying their theft, they were busily eating out his insides. But he managed to maintain his stoic posture through it all, never once revealing the pain he was in.

The trajectory of these myths led to two of my major adult beliefs: that I always had to take care of others' needs at the expense of my own, even to the point of losing a simple awareness of my own, and that I would not, indeed, could not, show my own pain or need to others.

It is not surprising, then, that this introduction has been the hardest to write. Giving myself nurturing and allowing and seeking support are still issues in my middle adulthood. While I have perhaps gained some insight along the road, self-nurturing and openly acknowledging my need for others can still feel shameful to me. Yet "where we stumble, there is the gold." I know in my heart of hearts that my struggles and, perhaps, my greatest successes and most important life lessons have been to love myself and reach out for help.

The quote on the title page for this chapter, "I have found God in myself and I loved her fiercely," was an opening to self-love for me. It leapt out at me a number of years ago, before I had even an inkling of feminist theology, just after I, the only woman in my class, had finished three years of intensive study at a Roman Catholic seminary. Once I began meditating on God/dess as being deep in me, of being part of me, my life began to change, a change that led me out of several churches, out of a job, out of a marriage— into my own spiritual power at the center of my life.

It is now slowly leading me toward allowing myself the support of other people, particularly women. Part of this path has been my need to redefine strength, not as "going it alone," but as being open and vulnerable. In her poem "A Strong Woman", Marge Piercy, one of my favorite poets and novelists, redefines strength:

> *A strong woman is a woman who loves*
> *strongly and weeps strongly and is strongly*
> *terrified and has strong needs....*

She continues:

> *What comforts her is others loving*
> *her equally for the strength and for the weakness*
> *from which it issues....*
> *Strong is what we make*
> *each other. Until we are all strong together,*
> *a strong woman is a woman strongly afraid.*[1]

This chapter will give you a chance to examine your own life, to see how and if you are nurturing yourself and what kind of a support system you have for your own growth. May we rise to the poet's challenge of being strong in word and action, connection and feeling.

WEEK ONE

Breaking down fences

Are you cutting off potential support
because of "old baggage?"

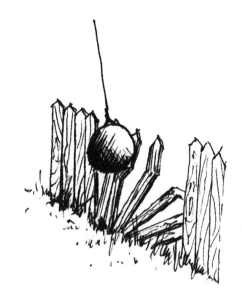

"Open sesame"
June 2, 1996

Just a few short weeks into my Jubilee Year I took a mini-vacation at the coast. One of my treats each morning was a walk to the Cosmos Cafe, where I enjoyed my first cup of coffee by a window overlooking the ocean. One particular day, I decided to take the direct route along the business section on the way back, rather than detour down the beach as I usually did. I was in a bit of a hurry; it was almost time to pack up and head for home. But, nonetheless, I stopped for a moment to watch an older woman kneeling on the sidewalk, small poodle beside her and paint brush in hand, busy at work on the front of a store that had had a "for sale" sign in the window for some time.

I said hello, then started talking to the dog. Pretty soon the proud new owner of the building and I were in conversation. She asked me where I was from and what I did. "Well," I paused for a moment, not yet able to answer this in one or two words, "I'm in transition. I was a counselor — now I'm getting into gardening and horticulture."

The next thing I knew we were on her flat roof, looking at her plans for a rooftop garden and deep into gardening talk. The zephyr wind ruffled our hair and the sun danced off the ocean waves visible from the rooftop as we created pictures with words.

"What about a clematis here?" Magically a purple clematis with large blossoms sprang up before us.

"No!" she countered "Too much wind up here." So we turned it into a rambling rose, then a honeysuckle.

Soon she was showing me the apartments she was refurbishing which opened onto the rooftop garden. By the time I left, I had an open invitation to return to watch the progress of this hidden hideaway.

A few months before, this encounter might not have happened. I would have been more guarded, more careful. It reminds me of a story I heard about a man going to heaven. As he entered, he saw a compound to his right, surrounded by high walls. Curious, he asked, "Who lives in there?" The punch line varies depending on one's own belief, but goes something like this: "The _____s. They think they're the only ones here."

For much of my life, if I were to be totally honest, I would have to say that I saw myself as one of the elect few who lived inside those tall fortress walls, quite sure that I was a member of the elite. I had cut the world into two — "them and us"— whatever "them and us" meant to me at the moment. I would have wondered whether this woman was too conservative, the wrong political party, anti-gay, not a feminist — and I would have had to check it all out before proceeding beyond simply courtesy.

But now I'm a gardener. I know that plants grow where they please, respecting no artificial boundaries. And I know that when I say the magic words, "I'm a gardener," it's like saying "Open Sesame"; people's hearts and homes open up to me, showing me their previously hidden and always magical kingdoms. Of course those kingdoms were there all along, just waiting for the secret password and my own open heart.

EXERCISE

• JOURNAL

Make a list of people and things outside yourself you have judgments about. In *You'll See It When You Believe It*[2], Wayne Dyer says that when we judge others, we do not define them, we define ourselves — we say more about ourselves and our own need to judge than we do about the other person. Perhaps there is something about the other person we refuse to acknowledge in ourselves. He suggests being more interested in why we feel judgmental than in "what's wrong" with the other person.

Pick several people you have "cut off." Write about why you did so, and what it may reveal about you.

• INNER WORK

In prayer and meditation, surrender all judgments to the higher power. Be willing to reopen to innocence.

• EXERCISE

Talk to someone or go someplace that opens a door you have shut. See what's on the other side.

• YEAR OF JUBILEE COLLAGE

Find something that represents unity, compassion, being beyond judgment (e.g., yin and yang, earth, cosmos) and place it on your collage.

NOTES

WEEK TWO

Me first!

Love yourself — the rest will follow

Soils
December 10, 1996

Yesterday I took my finals in Soils and Integrated Pest Management, then turned in three Integrated Pest Management reports; how plant health care resembles IPM, how to control dandelions in a rose bed, and how to control wild oats in an annual rye field. The quarter is just about over.

Of all the classes in my horticulture program, Soils has been my most difficult. It seemed drier and more technical than Tree Identification, or even Plant Science. But soils are really the foundation of all life on earth. They provide the growing plant with water, air, the right temperature for growth, nutrients and support. It takes literally centuries for climate and living organisms to act on rock, weathering it into small particles which will mix with decaying organic material, to even begin to create soil.

And yet soil can be destroyed in a matter of moments, days, a single growing season — the work of centuries erased by careless mistake, neglect or natural catastrophe. The only way to keep soil fertile is to constantly replace organic matter, the once living material whose decomposition by bacteria and other organisms constantly releases nutrients into the soil. If plants are not fed regularly they will be less and less productive, until the harvest becomes too small to make it worth the farmer's while.

I appreciate the often overworked and neglected soils right now. I've been using up the nutrients in my own life-sustaining soil the last quarter — through work, school, studies, worry about the impending divorce. I feel depleted, worn out. It's time to replace the old soil with new organic matter, plow it in and let it rest awhile before I try to plant a new crop.

I need to relax, that's for sure, over the one-month break before the next semester — watch a few movies and read a mystery novel or two. But even more important will be replenishing my essential nutrients with things that don't just busy my mind but feed my soul — walking, listening to music, meditating, seeing friends, reading inspiring books. I have a month to do this before I plant my "new crop" in January — Soils II, Irrigation Systems, Arboriculture I, Careers in Horticulture, Windows 3.1 Lab, and Landscape Planning.

"Leibig's Law of the Minimum"
December 11, 1996

I got my score this morning for the Soil comprehensive I took yesterday — 97%! Yeah!

I've studied hard this semester — now it's time for something else. It reminds me of another concept from soils and plant science: "Leibig's law of the minimum." There are 16-20 essential elements necessary for plant nutrition, and "Leibig's law of the minimum" states that plant growth is governed by the essential element that is in the least amount. This means that, even if there is an abundance of all other essential nutrients, their availability to the plant will be limited by the least-available nutrient.

It continued my line of thought from yesterday — the need to replenish the nutrients and organic matter in the soil in order to continue to have good crops. Especially the least available nutrient. From a human perspective, this law teaches me the importance of identifying for myself my "essential elements" and seeing which ones are in short supply.

I've had study, work and tight routine the past twelve weeks. I need to spend this month writing, reading, meditating, exploring spirituality, and just plain having fun; those have been my least available elements this past semester. I know I won't be able to fully avail myself of school and my studies next semester until I replenish those missing nutrients.

"I will arise and go now..."
December 28, 1996

After three days of Christmas celebration spent with family, I could hardly wait to get home. Now, here I am, my partner, Vilik, gone for a few weeks, alone in my own space. The rain is falling outside; the string of miniature white Christmas light bulbs is softly lighting up my plant corner. I am content, peaceful, deeply satisfied with my own company, which I prefer now to that of another. For a brief moment there was a flurry of snow this afternoon and I longed for it to keep falling, insulating me, isolating me in a soft cocoon of magic and promise and rest.

The evening flies by. I have a ham, pea and potato casserole and salad, watch some TV, but mostly spend the time typing my journal entries onto the computer, a hermit with a twentieth-century writing instrument.

As I snuggle into myself, I call to mind one of my favorite poems, "The Lake Isle of Innisfree," which I memorized long ago because of its beauty and message:

I will arise and go now, and go to Innisfree,
And a small cabin build there, of clay and wattles made:
Nine bean-rows will I have there, a hive for the honeybee,
And live alone in the bee-loud glade.[3]

— *William Butler Yeats*

My little apartment is, for now, my bee-loud glade, where "peace comes dropping slow." It will be hard to return to the busyness of school, of a relationship, of jobs. I just want to stay here alone, my spirit healing in the gentle, chosen silence.

EXERCISE

• JOURNAL

List some things you experience as self-nurturing. Why aren't you doing them or doing them enough?

• INNER WORK

In *Loving-kindness*[4], Susan Salzberg, an American Buddhist teacher, has several meditation techniques to help develop a deeper love of self. She suggests beginning by contemplating your own inner goodness and wish for happiness, then finding several sentences that verbalize your deepest desires and repeating them to yourself.

She also gives a meta meditation, originally taught by the Buddha. (Meta translates as "love" or "lovingkindness.") The meditation consists of mediating on four phrases:

> *May I be free from danger.*
> *May I have mental happiness.*
> *May I have physical happiness.*
> *May I have ease of well-being.*

In prayer or meditation, "sit with" these four phrases for awhile.

• EXERCISE

Each day pick one do-able item from your journal list. Do it. Push your limits about time (e.g., spend a little more time on it than you think is comfortable or "earned").

• YEAR OF JUBILEE COLLAGE

Find a small mirror and put it on your collage. Write on or around it something affirming about yourself.

WEEK THREE

No woman is an island...

Are you trying to "go it alone" more than you need to?

"The Bean Trees"

February 25, 1997

Evening: I've been sick the last few days. I finally "gave in" yesterday morning, came home, climbed into bed and canceled all my appointments, including class. I'm on herbal lung formula, aspirin, Nyquil, Contac, Neosynephrine, cherry cough syrup, cayenne, ginger, garlic, extra vitamin C, teas, bland steamed veggie and fruit juice diet, and I still keep coughing.

My horticulture professor called me this morning in response to my phone message about missing class. He told me not to worry about a thing, just to stay in bed and get well. Vilik went out and bought me food and medicine and made dinner while Flame, our new dog, lay next to me in bed. My landlord offered to come by and bring the amended lease, which includes the dog. And, just a few minutes ago, a classmate called to see how I was doing and let me know I could use her class notes to get back on track when I return to school.

So much of the time I try to go it alone, to be the caregiver, the worker, the perfect student. It's hard to let go and realize how much I sometimes need other people to help me. I have a very high tolerance for my own stupidity in that regard....

All this solicitude reminds me of one of my favorite books, Barbara Kingsolver's *The Bean Trees*[5], a novel graphically illustrating the interdependence of all people. Her main metaphor for the interrelationships of the characters in this story is one dear to my horticultural heart, the life cycle of the wisteria, one of my favorite vines:

> *Wisteria, like other legumes, often thrive in poor soil…. Their secret is something called rhizobia. These are microscopic bugs that live underground in little knots on the roots. They suck nitrogen gas right out of the soil and turn it into fertilizer for the plant.*

The rhizobia are not actually part of the plant, they are separate creatures, but they always live with legumes — a kind of underground railroad moving up and down the roots….

The main character, Taylor Greer, tries to explain this phenomenon to her newly adopted three-year-old daughter, Turtle:

> *It's like this…. There's a whole invisible system, for helping out the plant that you'd never guess was there…. The wisteria vines on their own would just barely get by…but put them together with rhizobia and they make miracles.*

Next Morning: In spite of my support, evening found me much sicker. I kept coughing and couldn't even move. I started to get scared, not knowing if I was going to get better. My partner called Silent Unity while I lay on the bed, crying. A man I never met, in a small room in the darkness of Lee Summit, Missouri, prayed for my healing while I silently listened, having no energy to respond. And suddenly I just let go — of my fear, my uncertainty, my need to control, my isolation — and everything was all right. Just like the wisteria vine, I had people in my life supporting me, helping to feed me, and with this "whole invisible system" holding me up, I fell into a deep, restful sleep and started my journey back to the land of the living.

EXERCISE

• JOURNAL

Write about whether it is harder for you to ask for support when you are "down" or "up." When you are down, who is there for you? How do you let your needs be known? How does shame block you from getting support?

• INNER WORK

In prayer or meditation, take your deepest shame to your higher power. Ask that you be shown yourself through the eyes of divine love.

• EXERCISE

Share a fear or reservation you have about yourself with another person — someone you haven't shared with deeply before.

• YEAR OF JUBILEE COLLAGE

Find or draw a picture that represents compassion shown by one person for another.

NOTES

WEEK FOUR

Allowing in "warm fuzzies"

Find your own cheering squad

"A Cloud of witnesses"
December 2, 1996

Yesterday was a true gift. My sermon at the Sunday service flowed beautifully. Literally dozens of people came up to me afterwards to thank me, saying they identified with my theme of being a "reluctant flyer," the biological description of the well-known plant pest, the green aphid. When I read that description the first time of these "crawlers and reluctant flyers," it seemed to be an encapsulated formula for the spiritual odyssey of the human race.

All weekend it seems people have been giving me compliments, everywhere I go. It was humbling at times, but it reminded me of a phrase from the Book of Revelation, "a cloud of witnesses." It refers to all the souls of the just from all time giving praise to God eternally. Through their acknowledging the creator of the universe, they found their whole beings filled with the spirit of truth and love, their own spiritual essence.

At church yesterday morning, still coming from a place where I have been judging myself so harshly, I had to trust that those acquaintances and friends, even some total strangers, caught a glimpse of me, the larger me, my spirit, my soul — a look that was truer and deeper than the distorted one I am carrying around right now. It brought to mind how important it is to have people in my life on a regular basis who, when all I can see is darkness and distortion, can reflect back a pure mirror image of my true self.

EXERCISE

• JOURNAL

What aspects of yourself do you allow to get support? What ones don't you? Where do you think people don't "see" you? Why? What would happen if they did? Do the people who surround you see your "small self" or your "big self?"

• INNER WORK

It has been said that, "False modesty is a slap in the face of the creator." Reflect on ways you have undersold or undervalued yourself. Is this really a true picture of your worth? In prayer or meditation, own and give thanks for the parts of you you're proud of.

• EXERCISE

Tell somebody something you're proud of — simply, directly, without apologizing or self-deprecation. Notice your feelings/thoughts and their response.

• YEAR OF JUBILEE COLLAGE

Draw or find a picture of some trait, accomplishment or action you're proud of.

CHAPTER FOUR ENDNOTES

1.   Piercy, Marge. "For Strong Women," from *The Moon is Always Female*. Alfred Knopf, Inc.: NY, 1980.

2.   Dyer, Wayne. *You'll See It When You Believe It: The Way to Your Personal Transformation*. William Morrow and Co. Inc.: NY, 1989.

3.   Yeats, William Butler. "The Lake Isle of Innisfree," from *Collected Poems*. NY: McMillan, 1956.

4.   Salzberg, Susan. *Loving-kindness: The Revolutionary Art of Happiness*. Shambhala: Boston, 1995.

5.   Kingsolver, Barbara. *The Bean Trees*. Harper and Row. NY: 1988.

NOTES

V

Constant Creation

*What occurs around you and within you reflects
your own mind, and shows the dream you are weaving.*

—Dhyani Ywahoo, Cherokee elder

Introduction

$\mathcal{T}$he ideas presented in this chapter are a cornerstone of this Year of Jubilee. If you "get" the ideas in this chapter, then your life really will change dramatically. If you don't, perhaps it will change in bits and pieces, but not completely, organically, wholly.

In this human drama into which we are born, most of us learn to believe, early on, that we are, in the deepest sense, helpless. As we grow older it becomes easier and easier to give the responsibility of our life, especially if it isn't "going right," to a force outside of ourselves — to other people, especially those in our family, the gods, the fates, our astrological sign, or pure random chance. This chapter's intention is to turn on end all those belief systems. It is not for the cowardly or faint of heart.

Deepak Chopra, in *The Seven Spiritual Laws of Success*[1], claims that each of us is nothing other than "the Self curving back within itself to experience Itself as spirit, mind, and physical matter." He goes further to state that all processes of creation are processes through which the Self or divinity expresses Itself. We are not the object of this process of life, but the subject. Knowing, in the most profound sense, that we are the authors of our own existence, allows us to fulfill any dream we have. We are truly eternal possibility, filled with immeasurable potential.

In *Conversations with God*[2], Neale Donald Walsch claims God revealed to him that "...if you are God's equal, that means nothing is being done to you — and all things are created by you. There can be no more victims and no more villains — only outcomes of your thought about a thing." He goes on to elaborate, stating that, "Nothing occurs in your life — nothing — which is not first a thought."

These eternal truths are like gravity, operating with or without our knowledge and consent. For millennia people didn't understand the law of gravity, yet they lived their lives under its rule. It wasn't until gravity was understood that we realized there was no point in denying that law, but understood that by working within its principles we could, in fact, fly. And as we understand the laws of the metaphysical as well as the physical world, we realize it becomes possible to consciously work with and use them, also, to fly.

Yet, many of us choose to defend to the death the right to be victims rather than even consider another way to envision our lives. What about sickness? What about death? What about the humdrum daily thoughts we have which, added up, over days, weeks, months, years, limit our imaginings and shorten our steps?

For the month it takes to work your way through this chapter on conscious creation, I offer you an opportunity to begin the process of literally "re-inventing" your life. Toss out the "could haves," "should haves," "if onlys," and "might haves," and claim for yourself your wildest dreams, your greatest thoughts, your most perfect *you*. If, in thirty days, you are not satisfied with the new you, then you can go back to the old one. What have you got to lose?

WEEK ONE

Metaphysics 101

What you "tune in to" becomes real in your world

The ether
June 15, 1996

When my older daughter sold me her 1990 Subaru Justy two years ago, she removed the radio. This week I finally got around to having it replaced. In a hurry, I drove away after it was installed without asking for instructions. How difficult could it be to turn a knob?

But somehow radio technology had bypassed me — I couldn't even figure out how to change stations. Every time I turned on my new radio I got a country western station, even though I longed for the classical music of public broadcasting. Well, when all else fails — read the instructions. It turned out my radio had a push button which, when punched, went on its own to the next station up the band. I pushed as fast as I could, until, at long last, opera burst from the speakers.

It made me reflect on all the other people driving by me, each one tuned into their own favorite station, dictated by their own unique taste. The air was actually filled with the waves of every station, but the miracle of technology made it possible for each of us to tune into only that station with which we resonated.

I thought about all those radio waves, totally surrounding us at all times, just waiting for us to plug in and turn them on. What a wide variety of choices, of music, of messages. It's like that with our beliefs, too. We all live in an ether which surrounds us, full of all sorts of ideas and beliefs, from fundamental Christianity to New Thought, from conservative to liberal, from self-destructive to self-affirming. Our biggest mistake is to think that the one channel we're tuned into represents all that's playing, and that we have no power to change the station.

Last month the only station I knew how to tune into was the "domestic violence and rape" station. That station seemed to be all that was playing, at least on my radio; it totally influenced the way I saw the world. But this month...this month I know I have choices. And this month I'm playing with those choices, turning to the "Gardening Tips" section of the newspaper rather than the police blotter, hanging pictures above my desk of trees and flowers rather than wanted felons.

The fact that I'm not tuned into the domestic violence station doesn't mean I don't care, that I'm not grateful for the dedicated people doing the work that needs to be done. But it also doesn't mean more domestic violence will occur if I don't tune in. I'm playing with my personal psychic radio, finding out what happens when I push another button and pick another station. Like the world of horticulture. Right now I'm enjoying this new "music," and I'm liking the way tuning to the world of nature softens and expands my view of the world.

EXERCISE

• JOURNAL

As your write this week, consider what "station" you usually listen to. Have you ever had occasion to switch channels? What precipitated that action? Sometimes there's "static"; the station we want seems too far away, or another station is in competition. What's the "static" on your radio? How can you "tune in" better and clear up reception?

• INNER WORK

In prayer or meditation, allow yourself to feel your own vibration, the resonance of your own energy, the "signal" you give out. Also allow yourself to experience what that vibration pulls toward you, and what it pushes away.

• EXERCISE

Find and read a basic book/article about metaphysics, creating your own reality (e.g. Abraham, Seth, Wayne Dyer. Check through bibliography for resources).

• YEAR OF JUBILEE COLLAGE

Draw a picture/design of how you experience your own vibration, and put it on your board.

NOTES

WEEK TWO

Manifesting takes time

Give your creations time to blossom

Psychic sunflowers — Part one

May 25, 1996

From the very first moment I saw the seed packet I knew I had to have them — Mexican sunflowers. Instead of single yellow-orange heads, those on the packet were multi-stemmed, bright red, all nodding gaily towards the sun. I knew exactly where they would go: the planting bed on the north of my property, up against a four-foot cedar fence and in back of the mixed salad greens — cos, romaine and redleaf lettuce, radishes, mustard, Italian dandelions, kale, corn salad, radicchio, celery, spinach, parsley.

Planning ahead, I sprouted the seeds in my small apartment, carefully turning on the fluorescent light before I went to work at seven in the morning and turning it off at midnight. Only I hadn't counted on the weeks and weeks of rain (so far the third rainiest year in Oregon's recorded history). This was great for salad greens, but not for sunflowers. The greens soon outstripped them, leaving their single little heads shaded by lettuce. Today, I noticed they were yellowed and drooped into the mud: not a promising picture.

Hopefully, the thinning of the covering plants, plus some new stock from my apartment window, will save my sunflower crop for the year. For every time I look toward the fence and my heart leaps, it isn't those poor straggly little seedlings I see at all. It's brilliant Mexican sunflowers, dancing in the sun.

Psychic sunflowers — Part two
July 30, 1996

It was sweltering yesterday, but it's already time to prepare for a fall garden. I got up early and went out to weed, thin, water and fertilize with horse manure from the county fairgrounds. I hope to plant more spinach, lettuce, snow peas, radishes, dandelions, mustard, kale, beets and carrots to take me into winter.

As I thinned out the salad greens plot, removing the bolted broccoli, mustard, radishes and kale, I exposed the back row next to the four-foot cedar fence. There, growing slowly but surely, was my row of Mexican sunflowers. A couple of spots were bare and some seedlings were still only a few inches tall, but others were over a foot, with tightly clustered heads that looked like they would open soon. I threw a few handfuls of manure and potting soil around their base, watered them deeply and smiled to myself, knowing my secret garden will be an eye-stopper and spirit-lifter in just a few days. The seeds I planted, even in the summer doldrums, even on my own days of depression, were planted with foresight, love and hope, and cannot help but blossom.

Psychic sunflowers — Part three
September 4, 1996

I spent both Saturday and Sunday in my soon-to-be new home, cleaning up the mess left by the former tenant. I vacuumed, dusted, steam cleaned the carpet, got the cat smell out of the bathroom, scrubbed the toilet, and defrosted and cleaned the refrigerator after throwing out the spoiled food. It all seemed to take forever. At one point, when I realized the carpet was still covered with pet hair even after being shampooed and felt ready to tear out my own hair as well, I wandered out into the yard and over to the north patch, the one with the Mexican sunflowers that had taken so long to bloom. I took a moment to savor the flower heads finally bursting into fiery bloom, before picking one out to go back with me to the chaos of my new apartment. There, enthroned in a glass vase, its cheery bright orange face with sunny yellow center encouraged me to keep going.

Monday afternoon I was actually able to move in my furniture and today, Tuesday, the house is beginning to take shape. My bed is a mattress on the floor, the platform to go under it resting beneath the outdoor steps, waiting my decision whether to go from a queen to a double. My books are still in haphazard boxes and the floor is littered with stray items with no home yet – a seashell, a marble, a bird's feather....

But it's coming. The bare walls are filling up in my mind's eye — the Georgia O'Keefe over my bed between the two windows, my fiftieth birthday collage next to the dining room table, my "Year of Jubilee" collage over my recliner in the living room.

I feel like Pygmalion, the ancient Greek sculptor who carved a woman out of stone and then watched her come to life. There's still a little more sculpting, and lots of polishing, to make this my new home, but it's happening. I am having my first cup of morning coffee at my dining room table right now, looking across at the simple beauty of my very own grown-from-seed Mexican sunflower.

EXERCISE

• JOURNAL

In *Conversations with God*[3], Walsch states that "nothing occurs in your life — nothing — which is not first a thought." Write about your reactions to and reflections on this idea.

• INNER WORK

In prayer or meditation, look carefully at the "seed thoughts" you have been planting. Which are "flowers" and which are "weeds"?

• EXERCISE

As you go through your week, see what "seeds" you want to plant in different situations and relationships in your life. Let yourself plant them.

• YEAR OF JUBILEE COLLAGE

Find a seed (e.g., sunflower, pumpkin, tomato, pepper), then draw/find a picture of the mature flower and mount them side by side.

WEEK THREE

But how could this happen to me?

You may be giving what you don't want
more attention than you realize

Here, kitty, kitty!
May 24, 1996

Meg, my 17-year-old, is down for the weekend. When we went out to shop,
I couldn't help but drop in on a pet store to visit the hedgehogs. I know someday,
somehow, I'll have one, even though my partner claims to have an allergy to them.
After a brief visit to the prickly little creatures, I was half-way out the door when Meg
called me back. "Mom, let's see the other animals."

I went back in, moving down the rows of cages quickly – it always makes me
sad to see animals in cages. But one black and white kitten caught my eye. She was
sitting there, eyes wide open, a little apprehensive. Above her was a large parrot in a
cage. The parrot was talking loudly, which, understandably, had the kitten on edge;
the parrot's seemingly human voice overturned the natural order of the universe.

It reminded me of a story I had heard about a lost parrot. The owner was frantic. When his friend tried to reassure him, claiming the parrot would eventually
return on its own or be found, the owner replied: "You don't understand! All it knows
how to say is 'Here, kitty, kitty!'"

Sometimes, like that lost parrot, I have little or no awareness of the power of
my thoughts, of my words, as they literally summon a situation or event that is not

the one I consciously want. As I watched that apprehensive kitty, I wondered what messages I now utter to myself without knowing or accepting their power.

I love the freedom of being self-employed, which, along with unemployment insurance as a safety net and summer coming up, is delightful. Yet already I can hear myself saying things like: "Well, I'll probably need a full-time job as someone's employee by next summer." "Most people in this business know a lot more about it than I do." "How can I get a loan for a used truck if I can't prove steady income?"

The kitten was having a bad day but, hopefully, someone would purchase her soon and take her to a loving home (probably without talking parrots). But I need to pay more attention to that voice in my own head, making sure it's really saying those things that will support me in my job, in my life, and not just parroting those old "here, kitty, kitty!" tapes.

EXERCISE

• JOURNAL

In *Conversations with God*[4], Walsch speaks of the Sponsoring Thought, the thought which underlies conscious thoughts. If it is out of alignment with our conscious thought, the Sponsoring Thought will always win.

Write about an area of your life in which your conscious thought is to have something which does not seem to be manifesting. Look deeper and see if you can find the Sponsoring Thought which may be tripping up your conscious intention.

• INNER WORK

Edgar Cayce, in *Your Life: Why It Is the Way It Is and What You Can Do About It*[5], claims that as you think about "that you dwell upon" or "that you hate," you put energy into your aura. "When you put it there, even though you may hate something, you'll attract it to you. So don't hate anything. Find something to like or to love. Let your mind dwell on that and build it for you." This allows what you love to come to you.

In prayer or meditation, go through troubling situations in your life and find something in each to like or love.

• EXERCISE

Notice how many times this week you are focusing on what you don't like or don't want. Notice what happens as you do that, the tension and closing of the heart. Also notice how you feel when you're focusing on something you like or love.

• YEAR OF JUBILEE COLLAGE

Put something on your collage that just makes you very happy when you look at it.

NOTES

WEEK FOUR

Believing is seeing

Make your dreams come true!

It's a truck!

January 26, 1997

Friday morning I was finally ready to tell the universe what I wanted — a truck, Nissan or Toyota, no more than 10 years old, extra cab, non-smoking owner, manual shift, AM-FM/cassette, bed liner, canopy, low mileage, good condition, for no more than $4,000. My first divorce payment is due on February 21st, $4,500 tax-free, and I want a truck and my first IRA out of it.

When I got out of my landscape planning lab early I had an impulse to ask Susan, one of my classmates, if she wanted to get a cup of coffee with me, something I had not done before. While we were visiting, I told her that I was in the market for a truck, describing to her exactly what I wanted. She told me she would keep her eyes open for me. Meanwhile, I just kept holding my vision out to the universe and allowing myself to be open to receive it.

Twenty-four hours later, Saturday afternoon, I found a message from Susan on my answering machine. That in itself was surprising, since I'm unlisted. A few weeks before, I had given Susan my new business card with my home phone number on it, and apparently she had held onto it. When I called back, she told me she had seen a Nissan truck near her house on her way home Friday with a "For Sale" sign on it.

I immediately called the owner. Yes it had an extra cab; no he didn't smoke; yes he was the original owner; yes it had a canopy, bed liner, AM/FM/cassette, and very low mileage (under 63,000). It was a 1985, but the low mileage and excellent condition more than made up for the year. And the clincher was that he couldn't actually sell it until his new truck arrived — the week I am due to get my check from Harry!

I made an appointment to test drive it today after church. It's a beautiful golden bronze, with a slightly lighter gold canopy. And it drives beautifully. No accidents or major dings, and it comes with a tool box in back, chains, extra filters, manual, and complete service records. And the owner wanted exactly $4,000 for it. I had checked the Kelley Blue Book on the Internet Friday night, to get some comparison costs; that model sells for an average of $5,000 on a used car lot.

I handed him a check of $200 earnest money, contingent on the truck passing inspection with my auto mechanic. I can't imagine it won't. Now I have a few weeks to sell my Subaru and get my first divorce payment ... just in time to pick up my dream truck.

Boy, if this is how conscious creation can work, the sky's the limit!

EXERCISE

• JOURNAL

Pick one dream you have and write about it. Describe everything, down to the most minute detail.

• INNER WORK

In prayer or meditation, look at the "fantasy" you have created in your journal. Check to make sure it doesn't conflict with any other desire that you hold. If it does, sit with the multiple desires and let them evolve into one. Take that one desire and visualize it; include everything — how it tastes, feels, sounds.

• EXERCISE

Everywhere you go this week, look for signs of your dream (for instance, if your dream is a new house, keep your eyes open as you look at houses this week for aspects you want in your own house).

• YEAR OF JUBILEE COLLAGE

Put up a picture on your collage which shows your dream in detail.

CHAPTER FIVE ENDNOTES

1.   Chopra, Deepak. *The Seven Spiritual Laws of Success: A Practical Guide to the Fulfillment of Your Dreams*. Amber-Allen Publishing Company: San Rafael, CA, 1994.

2.   Walsch, Neale Donald. *Conversations With God: An Uncommon Dialog*. G. P. Putnam and Sons: NY, 1996.

3.   ibid.

4.   ibid.

5.   Cayce, Edgar. *You'll See It When You Believe It*. William Morrow Company Inc: NY, 1989.

VI

Embracing Chaos

If you realize that all things change,
There is nothing you will try to hold on to.

—Tao Te Ching

Introduction

*T*his year has been a roller coaster. The higher the ride soared, the deeper the depression seemed to be that followed. Yes, I surrendered to change at the beginning of this Year of Jubilee. But sometimes I wonder: how much, how fast? The quicker my slalom down the hillside of change, the more I've hurtled into some very hard "trees." I've been through divorce, a major bout of depression, bronchitis for two months, a questionable mammogram in the midst of losing health insurance, and literally running out of money more than once.

As I picked myself up after each collision, I kept asking myself the questions I have yet to fully answer: "Do you really believe that the universe is abundant? Then why is your checking account below zero and why have you been denied credit?" "Do you really believe that you are always in connection with the source? Then why do you feel so alone, so isolated?"

At one point, after a particularly acrimonious mediation session regarding my divorce settlement, all I could do when I got home was crawl, fully clothed and without turning the water on, into my big, claw-footed bathtub. It was the only place in my apartment where I could be in complete darkness and just fold up into myself. It was hard to believe I could even keep functioning, much less believe I was loved and supported by a presence bigger than I could possibly imagine right then.

One evening, as I was trying to piece my life back together, I picked up the *Tao te Ching*[1] for some insight and came across the following passage:

> *Trying to control the future*
> *Is like trying to take the master carpenter's place.*
> *When you handle the master carpenter's tools,*
> *Chances are that you'll cut your hand.*

I realized that I had ended up sitting in that bathtub, pulling the darkness around me, because I really had cut my hands. It was time to let go and trust that something larger than my little self was at work. Perhaps I needed to be in the darkness, to not fight it, to trust that the dawn would come.

WEEK ONE

All who wander are not lost

Having let go of what was, you may find yourself
in a period of unknowing

Far from the hobbit-hole
May 10, 1996

Today, my partner's birthday, we visited the rhododendron garden in
Portland. As I pulled into the parking lot I saw a bumper sticker: "All who wander are
not lost," a line from J.R.R. Tolkien. It reminded me of his wonderful story, *The
Hobbit*[2], which opens:

> *In a hole in the ground there lived a hobbit. Not a nasty, dirty, wet hole,*
> *filled with the ends of worms and an oozy smell, nor yet a dry, bare,*
> *sandy hole with nothing in it to sit down on or to eat: it was a hobbit-*
> *hole, and that means comfort.*

This particular hobbit, Bilbo Baggins, was a very well-to-do hobbit, whose
people were considered very respectable:

> *Not only because most of them were rich, but also because they never had*
> *any adventures or did anything unexpected: you could tell what a Baggins*
> *would say on any question without the bother of asking him ....*

At the beginning of this tale, Baggins was a creature who liked his comfort. He lived an orderly, peaceful life in which the day revolved around frequent, regular and bountiful meals. Then, suddenly, against his will, through forces beyond his comprehension and stronger than his reticence, he was thrust out of his little underground hobbit hole into an adventure that would change his life and transform the world.

Many of us, like Baggins, just "settle in;" many more just "settle." This time, I have not settled. I have taken the risk; I have "wandered;" I have done and said "things altogether unexpected." Like Baggins, I finally realized there was no straight line from where I was to where I really wanted to go. I had to give up my hobbit hole. If I had not, I would have spent today at a desk like my old one in a windowless office, working and worrying.

Instead, I had the luxury of wandering among blooming rhododendrons and azaleas, both they and I soaking up the sun. For a quiet hour I conversed with a young squirrel whose worried mother kept rushing between me and her baby, driving it away from me with her harsh chatter, an early lesson in the dangers of trusting humans. As I sat next to the pond, a large brown nutria swam through the shore grass, encountering a majestic goose which darted its neck down and hissed a warning. I marveled at the way the water beaded on the heads of the mallards, noticed for the first time how their black back feathers curl up and back toward their heads.

I am not always sure of where I am going, or how. But this afternoon I knew for sure that, even though I may be wandering, I am not lost.

EXERCISE

• JOURNAL

By now, midway through the year, you've had a chance to begin to create and explore your dreams. Are you afraid of the "wandering" as you let go of one but have not fully manifested the other?

• INNER WORK

In prayer or meditation, surrender both your old and new realities to God, Goddess, all that is, your higher power, or whoever or however you imagine a greater sense of yourself.

• EXERCISE

When feeling too lost or overwhelmed, watch yourself as though you're watching another person. Rather than say, "I'm confused," say to yourself, "She's confused." Observe the change in self-perception as you become "the watcher" of your own experience.

• YEAR OF JUBILEE COLLAGE

Find a picture/object of something that has broken open and place it on your collage.

WEEK TWO

Getting stuck

Does it seem like you're paddling as hard as you can, but the boat isn't moving?

Off day
May 22, 1996

I've had a couple of "off" days where I've been uncomfortable in my own skin, impatient as people seem to wander unwittingly through my auric space. Maybe it's just the weather: the third wettest year in Oregon's recorded history. It rains not once, but literally a dozen, two dozen times a day.

This morning I got up early to walk and greet the day, puttered around my sopping wet garden (mostly picking slugs off my lettuce and dropping them in a container of salt). After that I went to the Master Gardener demo garden, where we planted borders of zinnias and marigolds.

Next stop was my gardening job, but as soon as I got there the heavens opened, drenching me. I had to postpone, for the second day in a row, my next project. Restless and out of sorts, I came back home and decided to tackle cleaning out a closet. I keep tripping over myself and misplacing the screwdriver; then I sawed the dowel rod the wrong length five times.

Maybe it's O.K. to just have an "off" day. Who's to say Jesus didn't? Or Buddha?

I turn to the *Tao te Ching*[3] for some insight, opening to Chapter 22:

If you want to become whole,
Let yourself be partial,
If you want to become straight,
Let yourself be crooked.
If you want to become full,
Let yourself be empty....

Maybe it's a day to be partial, to be crooked, to be empty. And maybe it's a day not to put a judgment on it and just let it be.

The doldrums
July 29, 1996

The heat has been in the high nineties, up past one hundred on occasion, the humidity almost as high. At home it was all I could do to keep my four plots watered. I should be watering more deeply, weeding, building trellises, adding more manure, but I'm at a complete standstill, just like the weather seems to be. I finished up my work at Cheryl's last Friday; I haven't started the new job yet.

Today promises to be another stupefying scorcher. I'm halfway through a very stringent eating regimen that may or may not work to bring down my blood pressure. I bought my new inkjet printer Saturday, but don't have the computer yet. At church, we've been told we'll have to wait to find out if we'll get the minister we want.

The garden also seems to be resting. No new plants right now — I have to plant for fall this week, but right now everything seems to be sleeping. The tomatoes are not quite ripe; I've had only one or two baby zucchini and a handful of beans.

It is the doldrums: a period of low spirit, sluggishness, inactivity. It's like the equatorial ocean regions noted for dead calms and light, fluctuating winds. But I know that there are strong currents under the surface of this stillness, that the plants in front of my eyes really are growing even if I can't detect it. And I know that there is some life stirring in me yet.

EXERCISE

• JOURNAL

Take a break this week. Read a mystery or romance, go to a movie. Let your mind take a vacation.

• INNER WORK

To prepare for prayer or meditation, reread *In Impossible Darkness* by Kim Rosen, page xxv. Then, imagine yourself in a cocoon, a beautiful, silken white "skin" protecting the molten darkness of your metamorphosis.

• EXERCISE

This week give yourself permission to do less than you think you should and do it less well than you think you should.

• YEAR OF JUBILEE COLLAGE

Put a picture of something resting or sleeping [or nothing] on your board.

NOTES

WEEK THREE

Loss is inevitable

You can't move forward without letting go

Laid bare
December 14, 1996

The last several days I've been helping Vilik get ready for a trip to Santa Cruz. We've made trips to the chiropractor and the optometrist, done loads of laundry, and run last-minute errands. This morning was a rush to the airport ... an hour late, since she had thought her departure time an hour later. By tipping a skycap and literally racing to the departure gate, we made it — two minutes before the scheduled take-off.

The last few weeks between us have been rocky — I've been depressed, not fully present, withdrawn and snappy. I've been preoccupied with the legal divorce from Harry and our conflict over the shared pension, and wondering how my future will unfold this coming fall.

I didn't get back to my apartment today until after dark, and spent what was left of the evening reading and listening to Christmas albums. I just finished reading a moving journal describing a year spent on a Maine farm, *Here and Nowhere Else*[4], by Jane Brox. The writer finally returns to the farm of her birth, where her aging parents are trying to keep up with its demanding crops of corn, apples and mixed vegetables. An entry made in winter caught my eye:

> *Sometimes I think we have too much time in winter. Too much time to mull over numbers. Time to consider our place. Time to exaggerate our fears the way reasonable people do during a sleepless night — there's a*

presence behind them, a presence in the shadows, and no way to return to
the journey of their dreams.

I've been feeling that inky black, insistent presence in my soul — ghostly shadows scaring me, loneliness stalking me down country lanes, tears trickling down my cheeks at odd moments. On the drive home tonight I was struck by the starkness of the leafless trees, their silhouettes outlined against the salmon-orange clouds. There were no leaves to hide them, no fields of flowers to distract the lonely travel-er's eye. Just the trees, solitary, silent, stern, branches etched with the cosmic artist's pen, bones laid bare, idiosyncrasies, defects, and, yes, strengths and simply dignity in plain sight.

I have been anxious all week about my partner leaving right now — all my "stuff" about loneliness, separation, intimacy, connection, the meaning of life churn-ing up in me with her being gone and the impending divorce from my husband, from whom I've been separated over ten years. The meaning of life seems turned on its end, leaving me hollow and empty at times, a cold wind blowing through my naked and defenseless soul.

Yet as I drove home in the gathering dusk, under the the stark simplicity of the winter sky, heading rapidly towards the longest night of the year, I found myself craving my own company more than anyone else's. My leaves have been stripped off this year, and I suspect I'm cold to the touch. Yet I'm beginning to perceive my own outline clearly against the winter sky, to sink my roots a little deeper into the earth under my feet. In the darkness and cold, I seek out the depths of my own soul.

Flood and fire
August 29, 1996

A chilly early morning walk today, the middle of the summer harvest. Tomatoes fire-truck red on the vines, cucumbers proliferating faster than mid-Eastern recipes, and zucchini...enough said. Turn your back on them for a moment and you have a blimp, a monstrosity that seems to have no growth limits. Sunflowers are still setting heads, but many aren't open yet and the summer days, still in the 80's by noon, are getting minutes lopped off at each end, sunrise and sunset on an inex-orably determined collision course with each other until the winter solstice, December 21, when they will begin to retreat with the same precise regularity.

My garden shares this confusion, this almost-too-small-to-be-measured change, summer to fall. There is just a waft of autumn in the air, a few trees already tinged with gold, a brisk breeze pushing the startled clouds across the calm summer sky. Squash and peppers are still setting fruit, the days still hot and long enough for them. My seedling winter garden is scattered, almost in hiding, among the gaudy and gangly summer plants — a row of carrots germinating under the leaves of almost full-grown beets, another patch just seeded, kept cool and dark under a layer of wet cardboard, a shade cloth in place a foot above.

I just heard on the news last night that this has been Oregon's worst fire season ever, following the wettest winter. At first I thought it odd and merely coincidental that both records would be shattered in the same year; then I learned that one actually caused the other. The long, extra wet rainy season made the sage and other desert brush grow to three times their normal size. When summer came and dried them out, there was three times as much fuel for the hungry fires to devour.

It is as if fire and flood are bound together, each needing the other, each feeding off the other, just as summer and autumn are enfolded, feeling both the fruition and the fall in each. It reminds me of the course of my life, the course of human life, with births and deaths not being the nice, neat beginning and endpoint of living, but inextricably interwoven.

I feel such gentle sadness about these late summer days. In the midst of life, of bountiful harvest, I have begun to sense the nagging tug of winter, of solitude, of death. Today, as I write this, I am stretched out next to a beautiful, meandering river. Vilik is upriver from me, sitting in her favorite spot on a shallow, flat rock, surrounded on both sides by a rapidly flowing creek. She is in her new purple chaise lounge, reading, absorbing one last summer day to store up for winter, her feet dangling in the shallows of the river. I want to pause this moment, to somehow stop time, now, as I watch the outline of her head surrounded by the solid green trees, her turquoise halter against the purple chair, her black shorts contrasting sharply with her only lightly tanned "Oregon" legs. But the river keeps rushing by, flowing to the ocean and into the fall, taking with it precious minutes of my life. Time does not stop here, even for a brief moment, even for me. And I feel like crying.

EXERCISE

• JOURNAL

As we move into accepting for ourselves the things we most deeply want, we also must let go of the things that no longer fit. What losses have you had or do you think you will be having? How do you feel about them?

• INNER WORK

In prayer or meditation, visualize yourself on a beach as the tide rolls in and out. As the tide comes in, it brings with it the treasures of your new life, leaving them at your feet, ready to be picked up. As it recedes, it takes with it the things you are letting go. There may be a sense of poignancy and nostalgia, even for things you didn't think you liked at all, but which have, nonetheless, become familiar friends. Take this time to write about and honor your grief. Remember it is important to understand how each cycle of the tide, each cycle of your life, is valid, even the ebb tides. The tide will always return, bringing with it new gifts from the sea.

• EXERCISE

This week allow yourself to feel and experience any sense of loss and grief that may be present.

• YEAR OF JUBILEE COLLAGE

Hang up a picture that represents your loss. In some way memorialize it (e.g., outline it in black, hang a black ribbon from it, put an "In memoriam" or "Rest in Peace" next to it.)

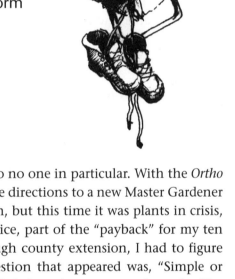

WEEK FOUR

Confusion or adventure?

If it keeps raining, start dancing in the storm

Chaos or kaleidoscope?
July 21, 1996

"How does this go?" I asked out loud, to no one in particular. With the *Ortho Problem Solver* at my elbow, I flipped through the directions to a new Master Gardener database system. I was a "hotline" worker again, but this time it was plants in crisis, not people. As a volunteer at the extension office, part of the "payback" for my ten days' worth of Master Gardener training through county extension, I had to figure out the computer software, fast. The first question that appeared was, "Simple or Complex?" Experimenting, I chose "Simple." It led me into one-word puzzles like "azalea, yellowing of..." or "coddling moth, identification and treatment...."

Apprehensively, I awaited my first phone call. Fortunately it fell into the "simple" category: "Clematis." Cradling the phone on my shoulder, I typed in the letters "c-l-e-m-a-t-i-s," bringing up several entries. At last the caller and I agreed that the most likely answer to the problem was too much moisture, due to our record-breaking rainfall this past winter. Relieved, I hung up to await the next call.

As I waited, I found myself wishing I had a database for my own life, something like, "Mary, meaning of." "Transplant shock" seemed to describe my condition a short month into my Year of Jubilee. Transplant shock occurs when a plant is uprooted, its roots broken off and water uptake system disrupted, the process of photosynthesis stopped, the respiratory system distressed. It is possible to minimize this by watering the plant heavily before transplanting, trimming back some outer growth, planting in the evening, covering it to slow down evaporation, keeping the soil moist, giving it time and checking on it regularly. With luck it will heal itself and adjust to its new surroundings. A living thing — plant, animal or person — isn't a light switch, turning on and off, but a life force with its own rhythms and patterns.

I suppose it's not surprising that I'm sort of "resting" now. I was transplanted, roughly, without warning, and with no care or forethought. But I'm here now, in one of my new locations, the orange plastic nametag on my T-shirt proclaiming, "Master Gardener, Benton County." I'm depressed at times, however, wondering if I can integrate all the changes I must go through fast enough to stay alive and begin setting down new roots. Sometimes my life feels chaotic, out of control.

"Chaos" is an Old English word originally meaning "to gape or howl." Formless matter and infinite space, extreme confusion and disorder. The first chapter, the first line, of Genesis, the first book of the Judaeo-Christian scriptures, the creation story, speaks of this word, "chaos:"

> *In the beginning God created the heavens and the earth. The earth was without form and void [in chaos], and darkness was upon the face of the deep. (Genesis 1:1)*

No reference points, no shape, no beginning or end. But then, in the second verse of the Bible, it goes on to state that "the Spirit of God was moving over the face of the waters." (Genesis 1:2) As the Spirit of God moved, chaos began to assume order.

A favorite childhood toy, one that would entertain me for hours on end, was my kaleidoscope. Each turn of the wrist worked wonders, bringing a new and beautiful reflection of order to the seemingly random collection of colored rocks. What would it be like to focus on the "chaos" in my life as possibility? What would it be like to see my life, which sometimes seems to "gape and howl," through a prism giving each new arrangement its own beauty? It was from chaos, after all, that God created all that is.

EXERCISE

• JOURNAL

You have come a long way; you still have a long way to go. But from here it would be as hard to turn back as it is to move forward. See your life this week, not in terms of gain or loss, but with a sense of adventure, of risk-taking, of boldness. Let yourself feel pride in the hard work you've done in the past six months. Make a list of all that you've accomplished.

• INNER WORK

In prayer or meditation, see yourself in a boat in the middle of the ocean, halfway between the shore you've left and the shore you're moving toward. Appreciate yourself for reaching the midway point, and being the bold adventurer you are.

• EXERCISE

When ships cross the equator they have a loud and noisy party. You are passing your own equator this week. Find a way to celebrate.

• YEAR OF JUBILEE COLLAGE

Put a big "6" on your board.

CHAPTER SIX ENDNOTES

1. *Tao te Ching.* Translated by Stephen Mitchell. Harper and Row, Publishers: NY, 1988.

2. Tolkein, J. R. R. *The Hobbit* (revised edition). Ballantine Books: NY, 1966.

3. *Tao te Ching.* op cit.

4. Brox, Jane. *Here and Nowhere Else.* Boston: Beacon Press, 1995.

VII

Joy in the Present Moment

Living is
a thing you do
now or never —
which are you?

—Piet Hein

Introduction

*I*t was a cold, wet winter morning. The alarm jarred me to begrudging consciousness, and I dreaded getting up and going out into the pre-dawn January day. Finally, dressed and shouldering my book bag for an early morning class, I opened the back door of my little apartment...to find myself facing an eastern sky burnt an umber so brilliant it seared my soul. As I warmed my car I looked again; it was just two minutes later, but the umber had softened, turning to wispy pink. And by the time I got to school the clouds had descended, turning the scintillating promise of dawn into a monotonous gray.

As I went to my class, I passed a fellow student who just had to stop me to share her joy. "Wasn't that a beautiful sunrise?"

All around me small clumps of soggy students were going through the motions of trying to wake up for eight o'clock classes, standing in line for espresso, eyes not yet quite focused. The miracle of this morning has obviously passed them by, but excitement danced in our eyes as my fellow-traveler and I shared our gratitude for those few moments of burnt-orange bliss.

I was reminded of that adage, "Carpe diem," come down to us as wisdom from another time and place, its demand clear. "Seize the day!" "Be present now!" "Be alert!" There is no passing this way again.

"Carpe diem." A spiritual practice of living in the present. "Carpe deum" is my own version. "Seize God/dess." Here and now, and nowhere else, we stand in the present, we stand in the presence of the holy, and by our attention we grab onto a bit of God/dess.

NOTES

WEEK ONE

Becoming empty, becoming ready

Forgive your past to come more fully into your present

The burning bowl
December 27, 1996

We had a cleansing and purification ceremony today at church. After writing down places in our lives where we needed to give or receive forgiveness we came forward, one at a time, to throw the pieces of paper into a fire. As the fragile papers burned, we let go of the things we had written on them, things that were standing in the way of living fully. I had listed the people in my life I still had tangled energy with, but I was struck even more by those I no longer needed to list. It gives me hope for what still remains.

There are many points of view about forgiveness. Some theories suggest it is the place to start, others the place to end. Still others imply it is not that important at all. It's certainly true that we need to honor our emotions, to acknowledge the grief and anger that have been part of our hurts. The child in us, especially, cannot move to forgiveness until we have heard and dealt with her experience and feelings. No timetable can be dictated for this process of emotional recovery; the journey is unique for each of us.

Still, and with all that said, I believe that an ultimate intention of forgiveness is not incongruous with feelings that may still need to be processed. There was a quote in the church bulletin this morning from the famous Persian mystic, Rumi, that reflected my personal view of forgiveness:

Out beyond ideas
of wrong and right
there is a field.
I'll meet you there.

However long and convoluted the journey, there is a destination, at least for me. It's the field that Rumi, the thirteenth-century Persian poet, proclaims — the field beyond the hurt, the resentment, the "being right." And I know that's where I'm heading.

EXERCISE

• JOURNAL

Make a list of people and incidents in your life that stand between you and your "field beyond." How important do you think forgiveness is in the healing process?

• INNER WORK

In prayer or meditation, choose a person from the above list you have offended. Recall the situation, the feelings. Ask and receive their forgiveness. Then choose a person who hurt you. Recall this experience, and then allow yourself to forgive. See the other person receive it.

• EXERCISE

Build a "bridge" this week. Write a letter, make a phone call, take the first step back towards someone or something you cut off.

• YEAR OF JUBILEE COLLAGE

Find/draw a picture of a bridge or outstretched hand.

WEEK TWO

The future is just a dream

Stop waiting; start living

"I have an appointment with spring"
May 13, 1996

The rain has been falling steadily all day, a soft, gentle, warm spring rain that opens up the sweet smells of the earth. I managed to get in a few of my own gardening chores during the sporadic lulls. Right before dinner I checked out the last plot, a corner seeded for beauty alone — clary sage and coreopsis, not yet broken free of the seed coats holding their new life inside. Suddenly the steady drip turned into a downpour, but instead of rushing back inside to the warmth of my cozy ground floor apartment, I sat down on the bole of a bigleaf maple, protected from the insistent rain by the tree's thick canopy.

I smelled the earth, rich, loamy, rife with promise of new life. I listened to the soft drops of rain as they landed on the leaves, an occasional droplet falling gently in my hair. I relaxed, focusing on my breathing, feeling the rough bark of the tree trunk lightly touching my back.

More out of force of habit than need to know, I found myself glancing down at my wrist to see what time it was. Ironically my wrist was bare, my watch waiting on the kitchen table, left there after a midafternoon bath. I laughed out loud, thinking of a card I bought recently that shows colorful wildflowers bordering a quotation from Henry David Thoreau. It proclaims: "I have an appointment with spring."

Every year at this time, and then again in early fall, I have said to myself: "During my last year of life I want to notice everything. I want to stand watch, silent sentinel to the unfolding of the season, day by day, flower by flower, leaf by leaf." That final year, I've been sure, I would not allow myself to get "busy" with the things that always seem more important — job, chores, my own pressing need for accomplishment.

For years I even worked in an office without outside windows, cut off from any awareness of the daily rhythm of life. Occasionally, after looking up at the large wall clock illuminated by harsh fluorescent lighting, I would take a "non-smoking break" — a chance to catch a brief glimpse of the sky, a quick, longing look at the changing season on the grounds of the county courthouse across the street. But there was no time to walk over and smell the flowers or touch the trees — I was too busy saving the world.

Exactly how was it going to be, I wondered today, as a furtive raindrop coursed down my back under my T-shirt, that I would actually know when my last season was? Would I get a written reminder from the universe? "Notice: This spring will be your last on earth. Enjoy it now, while you can."

And, suddenly, I was no longer a fifty-year-old woman. I was in my early twenties again, a young mother, at the hospital at the bedside of a cousin, a man in his fifties, a man I had known all my life. He and his wife lived at a residential treatment center for the mentally retarded and developmentally disabled, where he had been director for many years. It was a high-stress job with many responsibilities, but every summer for two weeks he would get away by donning his hunting vest, cleaning his high-powered rifle, loading his pickup truck, and heading for the hills.

The call to come to his bedside had come out of the blue. I found him lying under sterile white sheets, gaunt, wasted, dying, his dreams of a retirement where the dates of the hunting season rather than the dictates of a demanding job would have directed his days ripped away by the invasive cells of the illness. For him there would be no more wind blowing on his face as he examined the forest floor for signs of game, just pain pills and bedpans until his besieged body gave in to the invasive cancer whose arbitrary and merciless sentence was death. I had no words of wisdom for him as we shared the realization that he was dying, the understanding that this was our last moment together.

Back with my young family I threw myself into the demands of motherhood, trying to push from my mind the picture of him, helpless in a hospital bed, the sheets merely softening the outlines of the pain-wracked, wasted body.

I hadn't thought of him in years, but the memory of his death has been haunting me for weeks. Half a lifetime later, my children now grown, I can no longer afford to wait for that reminder I think the universe owes me, that year's warning I have somehow expected to have.

After one last look up into the young leaves of the bigleaf maple I stood up, shook the water from my hair, and came inside. As I opened the door I saw my forgotten watch sitting on the table, and was acutely aware, in that moment, that its steady progress forward offers no firm promise of tomorrows. If I am to have an appointment with spring, it can no longer be postponed. This spring, indeed, this day, this moment, is the only one I am certain I have. I have realized, this drizzly spring day, that God is here, now, and nowhere else.

"Only so many mornings..."
July 31, 1996

I planted the first of my fall crops this morning, then left for the county fair. I parked at the university so I could walk to the fair on the path that passes under the Irish Bend covered bridge. I regretted not having a water bottle, even for this short, twenty-minute walk; the noon sun, hot and dry, beat down on me. Even the llamas were in a far corner of the field, shaded by their outdoor, open-sided stalls.

An occasional biker or jogger sped past me. I commented to one, "I feel like a snail, I'm moving so slow." But I had my eyes wide open — open to see the shimmering mirage of the far end of the road, the distant hills changing perspective at every step. And I had my heart open — to feel the magnificent slowness of the still moments of noon, the preciousness of my own life, released into joy. It reminded me of a favorite poem of mine by Mary Oliver, "The Deer," written one day after observing deer in a meadow:

> *This is earnest work, each of us given*
> *only so many mornings to do it —*
> *to look around and love*
> *The oily fur of our lives,*
> *the hoof and grass-stained muzzle....*[1]

This is not a day I will look back with regret, regret for not looking around and loving. What more is there?

EXERCISE

• JOURNAL

List all the things, big and small, that it "would break your heart" to die and never have done.

• INNER WORK

In prayer or meditation, create your "perfect day" and live it through in a visualization.

• EXERCISE

Do one thing this week you've always wanted to do and never done.

• YEAR OF JUBILEE COLLAGE

Put something on your board that elates your spirit, makes you happy to be alive.

WEEK THREE

Play, play, play!

Your life is a playground — enjoy yourself!

Putting joy first
May 4, 1996

I got up at seven this morning to take a walk through the sleeping neighborhood. When I came back, I began a planting in my self-designed and self-built raised bed, filled now with soil composted with horse manure I hauled from the county fairground. As I looked up from my work, I noticed two of my neighbors leaving for an all-day volunteer training at the agency that so recently fired me. Knowing that a few short weeks ago I, the person who led the trainings, would have had to leave even earlier, prepared to spend all day in a windowless room, only added to the sweetness of my morning.

I marked off the beds, biodegradable twine outlining my square-foot garden: mizuna, lettuce, beets, kohlrabi, dandelion greens, pepper cress, chives, onions, carrots, beets, radishes, kale, corn salad, parsley, nasturtiums and marigolds. I drew the furrow in the soil with my forefinger and sprinkled the seeds in, lightly collapsing the furrows over them. It may still look like just a patch of brown dirt but I have gardener's eyes, eyes that see beneath the soil as water and the sun's warmth work their magic. In my vision swollen seeds are already bursting from their coats, leaves are reaching for the sun, and roots are breaking through clods of dirt in search of food and water.

This is the joy here, now: the present moment. What is sown today, not only as seed, but as thought and word, will come to harvest in its own time, given the room to grow. I told myself at the beginning of this Year of Jubilee I would place joy first, and it's happening!

"I will be the gladdest thing under the sun..."
May 14, 1996

It was a slow day at work. My back was protesting a bit; a steady spring rain fell. Having a little free time in the afternoon, I flipped through a gardening magazine to find this compelling poem by Edna St. Vincent Millay[2]:

Afternoon on a Hill

I will be the gladdest thing
Under the sun
I will touch a hundred flowers
And not pick one.

I will look at cliffs and clouds
With quiet eyes,
Watch the wind bow down the grass,
And the grass rise.

And when lights begin to show
Up from the town,
I will mark which much be mine,
And then start down!

Yes, slowly, day by day, I am learning it is possible to be "the happiest thing under the sun," to follow my joy, to become my joy, to live the exclamation marks St. Vincent Millay uses to convey her happiness.

"Shut up and dance!"
October 1, 1996

I left for school fifteen minutes early, after digging up a few more complete samples of weeds for an assignment — penny cress, mayweed chamomile, everlasting peavine. A long line of commuter traffic headed into Corvallis as I drove out, but I made a U-turn at the golf course and "bagged" a chicory (well, maybe it's a wild aster, which I already have), then got a small cattail, including the roots, in a drainage ditch at school.

On the way to school I saw a great bumper sticker: "Shut up and dance!" Yes. Stop bitching and start dancing. This dance of life isn't a dirge, a funeral procession, but a spritely dancing to the music of my soul.

So I danced all day. Yes, I was in school because I wanted to be there – I was learning what I yearn to know. I got to walk around campus for lab and identify black cottonwood, cedar, Doug-fir, arborvitae, white pine, European ash.

Then Vilik and I took a ride in the country, letting our playful spirits lead. We went to a flower farm, where she picked a bouquet, and I wandered around to dig up more weeds with a shovel left lying there among the rows.

On our way home we stopped at a nursery where I found a few more weeds coming up between flats of unsold and dying summer flowers, and snagged a hanging basket of purple evolvularias and red impatiens, now hanging high up in my bay window.

This evening we spent lying on the bed grading papers (one of our part-time jobs), laughing together at some of the unintentionally funny sentences. After a sit-com, we crawled into bed and snuggled.

Yes, I followed that car's advice today. I shut up and danced!

EXERCISE

• JOURNAL

Do your journaling this week in your opposite hand — let your inner child tell you how she'd like to play.

• INNER WORK

In prayer or meditation, allow yourself to be "taken care of." Someone else is paying the bills, going to work, preparing your dinner, whatever tasks that consume your normal workday. You are to simply be...joyful, unencumbered, playful. Let your spirit wander where it will.

• EXERCISE

Go to a toy or variety store, and buy a toy your inner child wants. Play with it.

• YEAR OF JUBILEE COLLAGE

Draw/find a picture of a child playing or a child's toy.

WEEK FOUR

The sacredness of daily life

Take time to experience the holiness in all things

Pure joy
October 17, 1996

I love this time of day, the early morning — not yet light, air damp and heavy, sky just beginning to soften, sun tucked away under the edge of the eastern hills. I try to get up to savor these moments, before the concerns and chores of the day come crashing in on me. It's a time of pure being, not doing, and I savor it all the more because of all the projects that start so soon and usually take me far into the night — classes, study, work-study, landscaping, gardening, grading papers for extra income, taking time for friends and family. This early morning time is just for me.

On the way to school I will do what I always do, turn on the tape I keep in my tape deck, a Gregorian chant that just keeps repeating "Alleluia" over and over again. Women's voices predominate; the men's are softer, in the background. I have learned to sing the harmony, so all the way to school I sing out, focusing on the powerful, compelling music but more importantly, its message: praise, joy, being at one with all that is.

As I drive east, facing the hills, I witness the sun breaking its bonds, the mist rising off the pastures, the sheep grazing on the wet grass, the birds beginning to wake up — and I know, without a doubt, that this is absolutely the most important thing I do today, every day, the most important thing that I am, my singing "Alleluia."

A gardener's prayer beads
May 17, 1996

"So, mom, did you get to sleep in today?" my daughter, Ann, asked me on her birthday a couple of days ago.

"No, " I answered. "I like to get up when the day is young."

It's hard to explain that I need to check up on, or more precisely check in on, my garden. Has anything sprouted? Any pests still lurking around, hoping for a more sluggish gardener than I, before they return to their hiding places for the day? But it's here I touch down, root myself, gather my energy for the day's demands. I hold this time close to my heart, rubbing the minutes between my fingers, treasuring their smooth, cold feel, my own private "Ave Marias" to the blessed dawn.

I found a writing from a fellow gardener that captures this fleeting but foundational moment in my day:

> When...I go out into my garden before anyone is awake, I go for the time
> being into perfect happiness....The fair face of every flower salutes me
> with a silent joy that fills me with infinite content. (Celia Thaxter)

Practicing the presence [presents/present]
September 7, 1996

Yesterday evening I visited my soon-to-be ex-husband, Harry, and my daughter, Meg, in McMinnville, a town an hour away. On the way there I noticed a hawk perched on a tree, looking down and searching the roadside grass for prey, its whole being focused on that one moment. I realized suddenly how much energy I've wasted this past week, projecting myself into the future and worrying. "Will I have enough gardening work...be able to get work/study...move into my apartment before school starts...have enough time for work, study and family...be able to afford a vacation...."

It hasn't helped; all it's done is take me out of the moment. The hawk's fierce attention was my wake-up call. I need to move through the next few weeks a step at a time, staying in the present, "practicing the presence."

"Practicing the presence" is an ancient spiritual idea that suggests we call to mind, moment by moment, the presence of the holy. It makes me think, too, of "presents" in the sense of gifts, the many gifts of life that fill the time from birth to death and beyond. "Practicing the presents" came to me as my own form of meditation, a practice of being aware of the gift this life is and being grateful for it, right here and right now.

On the way home last night I could only find country western stations, so I finally gave in and listened. The first song was called "If Tomorrow Never Comes." It was the story of a man thinking of his love for his woman, how it was so important to give and receive love in the here and now, for tomorrow may never come.

So, my lesson this week is simply to practice the presence of the holy, practice living in the present moment, practice awareness of the present of life itself.

The importance of llamas (and lamas) in the city
June 8, 1996

"I want to go for a walk, Mary. Do you know a place?" Vilik asked me for the two hundredth time since we moved to Corvallis. Neither of us had yet found a satisfactory answer, beyond, "Let's just walk around our neighborhood." Peaceful, yet predictable and unimaginative. But suddenly inspiration struck me. "Let's go to the road leading to the Irish Bend covered bridge."

We live in a university town, Corvallis, home of the Oregon State Beavers. The university has an intriguing history. Begun over a hundred years ago as a land grant college with an emphasis on agriculture, horticulture, veterinary medicine, 4-H and extension services, it gradually expanded its offerings to include literature, psychology and other more humanist and people-oriented professions. There are still, however, herds of cattle and flocks of sheep and llamas (are large groups of llamas herds or flocks?) on the edges of a more urbanized campus, with veterinary medicine and agricultural sciences still popular majors.

So we parked the car at the deserted county fairgrounds and crossed the busy highway, past the metal barrier excluding cars, onto the Irish Bend Road. On the left, in a grove of oak trees, still and inviting in the hot noontime sun, lingered the smell of cow manure, the cows themselves somewhere else at the moment. To the right, inquisitive long necks rising above the tall grass they were nibbling, were a couple dozen llamas, their pricked ears signaling their awareness of our presence.

A slight breeze combed the white clouds overhead as we walked down the middle of the road past the llamas, who fell into line and followed us to the end of their pasture, stopping when we did.

Soon we were at the crisply-painted white covered bridge, walking across its thick wooden planks, wondering where the town of Irish Bend was, if it still even existed, and how a bridge from there ended up spanning a small stream running through the campus.

But mostly we were looking and listening. Looking at the small stream flowing quietly over the water-rounded rocks, the white snowberries and wild blackberries blossoming, a wild columbine with one last purple blossom still hanging on. And listening — to the creek, the wind in the leaves, an occasional waft of conversation from the cyclists or walkers on the road. We had already wandered off onto a well-beaten path by the creek. As we stopped in the copse of trees next to the stream, it amazed me that a place this quiet and rustic could be right in the heart of the city. There was no rush, no other person, no time cards, just the heart beating, the mind quieting, the body healing, the stream flowing.

As we walked back to the car, refreshed by our few stolen minutes in paradise, a woodpecker kept flying in front of us, stopping briefly at each wooden fencepost to check it for a small insect snack. As I passed the llamas again, I gave them thanks, grateful for their presence in this city.

I was sad to leave this sanctuary, but it gave me pause to reflect how I need to make sure I keep that quiet space within me, to draw on, to retreat to. It's so easy fill up time with lists, errands, chores, recreation, TV, "zoning out." But the monastery does not make the monk, the lamasery does not make the lama, a peaceful place does not make a peaceful person.

Each of us has to take the time to create that sacred space, that holy time, even in the midst of our "busyness," of our seemingly never-ending "to-do" lists. But perhaps our "to-be" list should be just as important — "to be" quiet, observant, prayerful. For each of us is called to be our own monk, our own lama, our own explorers of the ever-present mysteries of the universe.

I, for one, am glad there are [l]lamas in the city. And I plan to be one of them.

EXERCISE

• JOURNAL

Write about the times/places in your life where you have felt a special connection to the "holy." Where is your "sacred space/place" now? Write your own "to be" list.

• INNER WORK

In prayer or meditation, design or create a refuge, a place of solace and rest, for yourself. Let yourself stay there and enjoy the peace.

• EXERCISE

There is a time-worn story about the monk who was still unenlightened. All he did each day was "Chop wood, carry water." One day he finally became enlightened and gained a following. A student then asked him what he now did all day. His answer was the same: "Chop wood, carry water." The only difference was that he did it with full intentionality and presence. Choose one of your daily activities (e.g., washing dishes, taking a bath, eating a meal) and do it with mindfulness and full presence.

• YEAR OF JUBILEE COLLAGE

Find/draw a picture of something "common" that has uncommon beauty when examined.

CHAPTER SEVEN ENDNOTES

1.   Oliver, Mary. "The Deer," from *New and Selected Poems*. Beacon Press: Boston, 1992.

2.   Millay, Edna St. Vincent. "Afternoon on a Hill," from *Collected Poems*. Harper and Row, Publishers: NY, 1956.

VIII

Surviving Change

There is a season for everything...
a time for giving birth, a time for dying....
A time for tears, a time for laughter;
a time for mourning, a time for dancing.

— Ecclesiastes 3

Introduction

*S*ometimes it seems that as soon as we get our lives working the way we want them to, something...or everything...changes. Change is the one universal, the one thing we can, without doubt, expect in our lives. Yet few of us easily accept change, much less embrace it. And who of us would actually seek to create it? Too often we prefer the spurious safety of routine and monotony to a life tipped upside down, emptied of its stale contents, a cornucopia waiting to be filled with gifts from the universe.

T. S. Eliot's poem, *The Love Song of J. Alfred Prufrock*[1], is a poignant reflection on a man growing old as he tries to keep his life the same, day after day:

> *For I have known them all already, known them all:*
> *Have known the evenings, mornings, afternoons,*
> *I have measured out my life with coffee spoons;*
> *I know the voices dying with a dying fall*
> *Beneath the music from a farther room.*

At one point Prufrock dares to question his measured-out existence:

> *Do I dare*
> *Disturb the universe?*
> *In a minute there is time*
> *For decisions and revisions which a minute will reverse.*

He goes even further in his fantasies, asking himself:

> *Would it have been worth it after all,*
> *After the cups, the marmalade, the tea...*
> *Would it have been worthwhile,*
> *To have bitten off the matter with a smile,*

To have squeezed the universe into a ball
To roll it toward some overwhelming question....

But ultimately he shrinks back, asking only small, mundane questions:

I grow old...I grow old...
I shall wear the bottoms of my trousers rolled.
Shall I part my hair behind? Do I dare to eat a peach?
I shall wear white flannel trousers, and walk upon the beach.
I have heard the mermaids singing, each to each.

I wonder what siren songs they would have invited him to sing with them? None, sadly, that he would ever know. His last words are, "I do not think they will sing to me." Having chosen such a small life, he is no longer capable of hearing anything beyond its narrow confines.

This chapter is about change. How do we view it? Can we ever learn to accept it, embrace it, seek it? Or will we simply go along, measuring our lives out in coffee spoons? Do we dare to do what Prufrock could not — "squeeze the universe into a ball" and roll it toward some overwhelming question? Because it is then, and only then, that we will hear the mermaids sing.

WEEK ONE

Deep roots, deep faith

Keeping your center in the storm

Windthrow
May 31, 1996

It has been another beautiful, languorous day at the coast. At the Oregon Coast Aquarium in Newport, I admired Keiko, killer whale extraordinaire and newest resident, and was happy to learn, along with the rest of the crowd, that the fungal infection on his tail fluke had improved. After wandering past the other exhibits, pausing, as always, at the brilliant and ephemeral jellyfish display, I decided to take a self-guided nature walk through the outdoor paths around the aquarium.

As I strolled along following the signs, I learned to identify rush, a shore-loving grasslike plant with tiny rust-colored clusters of flowers breaking out at the joints, as well as beach willow, tiny beach lupine, ash, Douglas-fir, western cedar, spruce, manzanita, birds feet trefoil, foxglove, kinnikinnik, ninebark, evergreen huckleberry, salal, wild strawberry, Pacific madrone, ceanothus. All day I practiced rolling the names over my tongue, shutting my eyes from time to time and conjuring up the plants before my mind's eye.

Towards evening I sat down to read a northwest plant book. As I read the section on Douglas-fir (not true firs, but *Pseudotsuga menziesii*), I came across a word new to me: "windthrow." The author explained how new tracts of land being opened up to housing have most of the trees removed, keeping only a few for looks and potential sales. Those few remaining trees, standing alone, more open to the elements, are prime targets for "windthrow" or uprooting by the next fierce storm. The image helped me understand this past month and why I have not succumbed to "windthrow" myself, but withstood the loss of my job with more equanimity than I would have previously suspected.

For some time before I was fired, I had been shifting my base of support, my "stand of trees", if you will, out, into an ever-increasing if sometimes threatening connection to people beyond the small, intense group of workmates and political comrades who had, until then, been my main source of support in both my personal and professional life. My "stand" had, indeed, grown into a veritable forest, and included people involved in New Thought teaching, the Unity movement, Master Gardening, landscaping in general, and a few others to boot.

When the storm finally came, stripping me of my immediate companion plants, I swayed in the fierce winds. Then I sent my roots wider, connecting even more tightly with my new support system.

The storm has not completely abated. Sometimes at night I can hear the wind howling through my branches, feel its chill. But when morning comes I am still standing tall. Through e-mail, phone, personal contact, church and classes I reach out, part now of a community of my own creation, one that buffers and supports me as I reach toward the sun.

"...her leaf shall be green"
November 4, 1996

I've been preoccupied with midterms this week; I keep trying to memorize the chemical formula for photosynthesis. Somehow carbon dioxide and water molecules, transformed by light energy through chlorophyll and enzymes, become a complex carbohydrate, forming the bottom of the food chain that keeps me and all other life on this planet alive. Hydrolysis, light reactions, dark reactions, ADP becoming ATP, becoming NADPH; capillary action, field capacity, saturated flow, formula for determining water percentage in soil, tensiometers; nymphs, larva, insect mouth parts, life cycles, orders of insects, grasshopper anatomy; *Davidia involucrata, Ulmus parvifolia, Abies pinsapo, Nyssa sylvatica.*

As full as my mind is as I try to hold onto all these facts, this is still the easiest part of my life right now. I know here in the classroom what I have to learn; I can focus on it, practice, take a test and emerge with a star or a happy face on my final exam.

But the rest of my life is shaky. I only managed to work for an hour on Tuesday before I got rained out. Depression has threatened to overwhelm me, and sometimes it's been hard to get to my jobs at all. I did finally confide in several of my clients, telling them about the divorce and my depression. At least I was able to be honest with them.

Yesterday I chose glass frames for my new prescription, then went to dinner. I felt so down by evening I played hooky from a board meeting and curled up under the covers by 7 p.m. As I lay in bed, I found myself thinking of a Biblical passage I had read recently:

> *Blessed is the one who trusts in the Lord,*
> *and whose hope the Lord is.*
> *For [s]he shall be as a tree planted by the waters*
> *and that spreadeth out her roots by the river,*
> *and shall not see when heat comes, but her leaf shall be green;*
> *and shall not be careful of the year of drought,*
> *neither shall cease from yielding fruit.*
>
> *(Jeremiah 17:7-8)*

I have been looking too much toward the external circumstances to dictate my mood. I need to "spread out my roots by the river", the river of my own soul, in order to survive this "year of drought". It is time to go deeper, as deep as the waters of spirit, and allow that healing water to flow through me, right out to the tips of my drooping and thirsty leaves.

EXERCISE

• JOURNAL

By now the changes you have been making in your life may have left you feeling alone, without familiar support. Write about the way the storm of change has impacted your life. What familiar supports are gone?

• INNER WORK

In prayer or meditation, visualize yourself as a tree. See the storm blowing through your branches. Picture your roots firmly imbedded in all that is, whatever image you have of something greater than yourself. Feel the strength and nourishment move up your roots and into your very being.

• EXERCISE

Check out a biography or autobiography or see a movie of someone you admire. See how they handled storms in their own lives.

• YEAR OF JUBILEE COLLAGE

Find and mount an image of your source.

WEEK TWO

Trust in the moment

All you need is provided — right now

Into the new dawn
October 26, 1996

The past few days have seemed endless. Day before yesterday I took my math placement test. I'm good at math, and I'll be very frustrated if I have to take a basic math class again. The test was computerized; the questions changed according to my correct or incorrect responses. I ended up going ahead from basic algebra, rather than back to basic arithmetic, and ended up somewhere in trigonometry. Sine, cosine, and tangent are absolutely the only terms I remember from trig, but I did remember a lot of algebra and geometry, so hopefully my test results will show I don't need to take math; I'll check in with a counselor on Tuesday to find out.

I've had to make so many appointments — optometrist, physician, dentist, mammography — things which have to be done before I lose my insurance. I feel a little overwhelmed by all the focus on my body and its possible problems.

The divorce and my feelings about it still weigh me down. Night before last I went back to visit the home I shared so many years with Harry. He was away for the evening, and I took the opportunity to go through the photo albums of the family. Then I went from room to room, remembering stories of the family, reliving the good memories each room held. At the end, after a few tears, I picked up a little earthen "gaia" goddess I had placed in each room to collect the memories and sprinkled tiny stars with blessings in a hidden place in each room. It was a way to honor my history there and to say goodbye to the house itself, the one I will still own with Harry until the divorce is finalized.

On the way home, the car "open door" warning buzzer wouldn't go off — a signal to me, I'm sure, about something, but I'm not sure what. It's been a hard, hard few weeks, dealing with the divorce, letting go over and over again, not knowing what's on the other side — for me, for the family, for me and Harry, for my income, for my career, for my retirement.

Yesterday morning I was mulling all this over as I drove to school. I left home especially early because I wanted to be first in line at the financial aid office, to handle the details of my student loan before class. It was still dark as I drove east, but I noticed an interesting phenomenon, one that had never registered before. It got lighter towards the west first, not the east where the sun actually rises. If I had trusted only my external senses it would have been tempting to turn the car around and head west, back toward what seemed to be the source of the light, rather than into the dark, ominous thunderclouds marching toward me over the mountains in the the east.

But I trusted my inner knowledge, deeper than my external senses, that I was going in the right direction. When the sun finally broke through the clouds, it proved I had been right; I was facing the dawn. I need to have that same certitude about moving into my own life, even when circumstances don't seem to validate my sense of where I'm going. I need to trust that, dark and forbidding as the horizon sometimes looks, I really am moving forward, into my own dawn.

EXERCISE

• JOURNAL

Marge Piercy, in her poem, "Vol de Nuit"[2] ("Night Flight") writes that love is "flying into the darkness to a place that may exist." Reflect on that in your journal this week.

• INNER WORK

In prayer or meditation, still yourself. Still your mind and your thoughts and simply be where you are, knowing that your inner compass is in your heart, not in your head.

• EXERCISE

Watch a sunrise this week.

• YEAR OF JUBILEE COLLAGE

Create a small art piece containing a heart and some representation of direction, e.g. a compass, magnet, sunrise, road map, store map which proclaims "You are here!"

NOTES

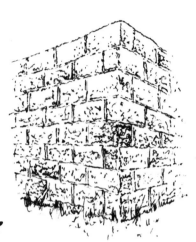

WEEK THREE

Keep moving, even if it isn't in a straight line

When your old ways don't work anymore, you can find new footing

Hitting the wall
July 20, 1996

For a year now I've been trying to lower my blood pressure with alternative methods like garlic, minerals, reduced salt. They haven't helped. Since I don't feel the symptoms and only see the problem when I take my blood pressure, it's easy to minimize or deny that hypertension is a problem. But two weeks ago my blood pressure reading of 190/130 was scaring me, and I opted to capitulate to pharmacology as well as additional dietary change.

Today, half a month later, I worked all morning in 100+ weather. I took my blood pressure when I got home; the reading hadn't gone down at all. I'm angry, sad, depressed, confused. Different people give me different information, sometimes the same people at different times. "Salt," "Some salt if it's 'good' salt," "No salt." I feel dehydrated almost all the time, especially when I sweat while working, and I need to drink great quantities of liquid, yet my doctor prescribed a medication that is a diuretic, further taking water from my already stressed system, lowering the volume of fluid in my arteries and veins, forcing them to constrict to conserve liquid. That sounds crazy to me.

I don't want to give up salt, carbonated beverages, occasional caffeine, most meat, junk food, quick food, tasty food. I'm trying to control my diet, but now I can't "reward" myself with food any more. I drive by "restaurant row" on the way home and find everything I desire — chocolate shake, barbecue, even a cola — not on my acceptable list. I feel trapped. A diet of fresh veggies, fruit and unsalted rice, beans and potatoes gets old fast. Why would I look forward to coming home to a bowl of organic brown rice, without even soy sauce since it has so much salt?

I hear my inner voices screaming out, "I'd rather be dead!" "I can't change!" "It isn't fair!" "I can't do any more than I am already doing!" And "What's the point of living anyway?"

After I took the upsetting reading this afternoon I got into a fight with Vilik, stomped out and ended up in a park next to the river, crying. After an hour AWOL I came home to share my feelings of sadness and frustration about my diet, which I had come to realize were being intensified by anxiety over changing to new landscaping job and client, and all the money fears that brought up.

As Vilik and I talked, I remembered a riddle my father posed to me as I was learning algebra. I can still see him, sitting in the blue armchair in the living room, while I sat at the dining room table, pen in hand, a blank sheet of paper in front of me. "If a frog is at the bottom of a large hole, 14 feet deep, and jumps up two feet at a time, but falls back one foot, how many jumps does it take him to clear the hole?"

Sometimes I feel a lot like that frog. Two jumps forward, one back. Once in awhile it seems like one jump forward and two jumps back. Today I slid down to the bottom of the hole. Again. I decided I needed to stop jumping for awhile, and take the afternoon off.

We went to our favorite park to try to cool off. I found an old apple tree off the path, set up my lawn chair, covered myself with a pink bedspread to protect myself from the flies, and just lay there since it was too sultry to sleep.

By evening I was ready to start hopping out of that particular hole — at least until the next meal with its challenges and frustrations. I have made two jumps back, but I'm still going to keep making those jumps forward.

Two steps at a time
June 1, 1996

My feet take me of their own accord to the edge of the ocean, whose retreating waves have uncovered rocks alive with sea life. In a moment I am on them, my tennis shoes wet, my eyes rapidly darting from pool to pool. Here an orange starfish. In that pool, the carapace of a Dungeness crab. And everywhere, tiny anemones, clumped together, leaving scarce foothold for me to place my feet.

Gingerly at first, not wanting either to step on more anemones than I have to or to slip and fall on the sharp rocks, I put one foot down and come to rest completely before venturing another step. But I soon learn that the trick is to be lighter on one's feet than that, not running, not looking further ahead than a yard or two, but to have each step flowing into the next — not static, not linear. Probably to a cliff watcher from above, my steps are sheer random, but dictated by a fluid, living, organic movement.

Testing my hypothesis, I leave the relative safety of the flattened rocks to try my hand — or, more accurately, my feet — at walking down the spine of a narrow thrust of rock twenty or thirty yards long. As my feet try my new two-step, my imagination dances along with them and I picture myself parading along the spine of a long-dead sea dragon. The "spine" disappears into the sand, and I jump off.

I understand that the lesson I just learned about gravity and motion is a lesson about life. No, life really doesn't go in a straight line, any more than my footsteps did through the tide pools. But going too slow can cause one to stop, and, in the very act of trying to find one's balance, one can lose the way.

EXERCISE

• JOURNAL

Is there some place in your life where you feel like you're going more backwards than forward? Write about how you are "stuck" there.

• INNER WORK

In prayer or meditation, "Let go and let God." Breathe deeply, relax all your muscles, let go your tension. Picture a beautiful bird, then picture that bird enclosed in a big bottle with a small neck. Feel its constriction, its folded wings, too confined to spread out. Now find a way for that bird to get out of the bottle without breaking it. (Meditate on this for awhile, then see the answer at the end of the chapter.*)

• EXERCISE

When you're going somewhere familiar this week, go a different way. Allow some time to encounter the unexpected.

• YEAR OF JUBILEE COLLAGE

Find or draw a picture of something "impossible," like a pig with wings, a dog on roller skates. Be creative.

WEEK FOUR

All roads lead home

No matter what it "looks" like, you can't really be lost

"Two Visions of Equal Force"
January 24, 1997

I went to the doctor's yesterday to have some moles and a cyst removed from my back and I returned today to have the wound repacked. As I was waiting for the doctor, the nurse handed me a copy of the reports on a mammogram I had last Tuesday: "Deep in the medial left breast...is an oblong low radio dense nodule with maximum dimension of 6 mm. This appears to be new.... In the lateral posterior right breast projection is a tear-dropped shaped low radio dense nodule measuring 8 mm in maximum dimension...Incomplete — needs additional evaluation."

I didn't have much reaction to it at first. In fact, the first mammogram I ever got seven years ago was suspect. I spent six months worrying about it before my next test showed no need for concern.

The doctor on call told me this new reading could be just fatty tissue. But another mammogram with a different kind of x-ray and a biopsy might be necessary if a six-month waiting period doesn't bring improvement. It wasn't until I was returning home late yesterday night that my mind started racing. What if...? What if the next mammogram can't rule out cancer? What if a biopsy reveals cancer? How will I cope? What about medical insurance? I'm still on Harry's, but that will end when the divorce is finalized. What will I live on? Who will take care of me? And on and on and on....

Then a short story by Bruce Catton, the great Civil War historian, came to mind. In *Two Visions of Equal Force*[3], he recounts an event which happened to him as a young boy when he and a companion ventured onto a frozen lake with ice skates and hand-held wooden frames covered with cloth which propelled them across the frozen lake. The day was perfect, the sun bright, the bare ice like polished steel, the sheet of ice stretching before them mile after frozen mile:

> *For a moment it was enough to be carried by the wind. The whole world had been made for our enjoyment. The sky was unstained blue, with white clouds dropping shadows now and then to race along with us, the hills that rimmed the lake were white with snow, gray and blue with bare tree trunks, clear gold in places where the wind had blown the snow away from sandy bluffs, the sun was a friendly weight on our shoulders, the wind was blowing harder and we were going faster than ever, and there was hardly a sound anywhere. I do not believe I have ever felt more completely in tune with the universe than I felt that morning on Crystal Lake. It was friendly. All of its secrets were good.*

Then suddenly everything shifted, revealing the darkness beneath their feet. They came to a broad stretch of sparkling, dazzling blue running from shore to shore, flecked with picturesque whitecaps — open water. Turning swiftly and casting aside the sails that were hurtling them to their deaths, they galloped, half skating, half running, to shore, barely outracing the cracking ice.

He contrasted this to a time a few years later when, as a teenager returning from a midnight Christmas service, he looked up to witness a host of golden stars whose bright flames denied the darkness. In that moment he knew that life was leading him somewhere, somehow, to a transfiguration.

Confronted with these two visions of equal force, one of darkness, one of light, he could not deny one to claim the other. With a wisdom beyond his years, he knew that each, in its own way, was true. He concluded that:

> *The worst and the best visions are true, and the ultimate truth that embraces both is fantastically beyond comprehension. Life is a flame burning in water, shining on a sea that has no shore, and far overhead there are other flames which we call stars.*

And for that moment, with those very same stars shining overhead, the mammogram report resting on the seat beside me, my own "open water" — I knew that, no matter what, I was on the way home.

EXERCISE

• JOURNAL

It has been proven that the first developmental stage an infant encounters is settling the basic question of "trust vs. mistrust." This life question keeps playing itself out throughout our entire lives. Is the universe trustworthy — or is it not? Are we safe here — or are we not? Journal this week about the early life decision you made. Have you had occasion or desire to change it?

• INNER WORK

In prayer or meditation allow yourself to know that whatever path you're on right now is just right.

• EXERCISE

If you are doing this Year of Jubilee with others, take turns going on a "blind trust walk." With the other person leading you, keep your eyes shut and experience trusting another being with your safety as you explore together your surroundings. If you are alone, you can do the same thing, possibly in your apartment or house. Move slowly, but trust your instincts of hearing and touch to keep you safe.

• YEAR OF JUBILEE COLLAGE

Put on your board something that represents your most negative experience; next to it put something that represents your most positive experience. Put a circle around them.

CHAPTER EIGHT ENDNOTES

1. Eliot, T. S., "The Love Song of J. Alfred Prufrock," from *Collected Poems 1909-1935*. Harcourt, Brace and World, Inc.: NY, 1936.

2. Piercy, Marge. *Circles in the Water: Selected Poems of Marge Piercy*. Alfred Knopf: NY, 1983.

3. Catton, Bruce, adapted from "The Joy Above the Stars, the Terror Below the Ice," in *Waiting for the Morning Train*. Doubleday and Co.: NY, 1972.

---

*Answer to riddle: Since you "imagined" the bird in the bottle in the first place, you can "imagine" it out the same way. Your obstacle was merely perceived as real.

NOTES

IX

It's My Life!

But little by little,
as you left their voices behind,
the stars began to burn
through the sheets of clouds,
and there was a new voice,
which you slowly
recognized as your own.

— Mary Oliver, "The Journey"

Introduction

*T*he "dead" of winter during my Jubilee Year provided me with time for reflection on my own separation, my own mortality. I was dealing with ongoing sickness in the form of a questionable mammogram and severe two-month-long bronchitis, along with divorce. During my December alone time, largely spent without the presence or support of my partner, I had many occasions to contemplate my own death. During that time I ran across a quote from *A Year in the Maine Wood*[1]:

> *The curse of consciousness is to see death, but it also sees the process of*
> *the whole. And the process makes each death less lonely, because life*
> *always continues into something else. It never dies.*

As I dealt with all the feelings and practical matters concerning my health and separation from a man who had been my husband for thirty-plus years, I had to slow down and be present in my feelings. What happens when we slow down enough to look under our "busy-ness?" What happens when we just sit still and stop hurrying? What still, quiet voice will we hear our authentic selves speak to us — in the silence in the center of our own lives?

WEEK ONE

Housecleaning

Emptying your "closets" of junk
is a good first step

"It is easier for a camel to pass through the eye of a needle..."
May 18, 1996

I have taken the day off to clean out my bookcases and files. As I begin this arduous task, I find myself thinking of a saying of Jesus: "It is easier for a camel to pass through the eye of a needle than for a rich man to enter the kingdom of Heaven." (Matthew 19:24) Some biblical scholars claim that Jesus was referring to the small Camel Gate in the walled city of Jerusalem, one where a weary wayfarer, coming to the city after nightfall when the gates were locked for protection, could pass through, but only after his camel was unpacked because the entryway was so small. Others claim it means exactly what it says.

No need to settle that biblical dispute now, but I am reminded of it whenever I look at a book or shuffle through an old file. Can I really throw away my articles on women's issues in the DSM-IV, or do I need to hold on? For what? Because someday I may decide to go back and get a doctorate in the social psychology of research methods? Highly unlikely. And how about those evaluation forms from a workshop I conducted on homophobia in Bozeman, Montana a number of years ago? Nope. Out they go, into a rapidly filling black plastic garbage bag.

The *Ancient Near East in Text* (ANET) and *The Ancient Near East in Pictures* (ANEP), however, give me pause. Remnants of my scriptural exegesis days at Mt.

Angel Seminary, they are too valuable to sell, so I put them on the pile to take to Harry's to store for a future date.

Maybe I need some basic domestic violence and sexual assault information, so I compromise here — keep one copy only, label them clearly and put them in a box to go under my bed. And so the day goes, book by book, file by file: each one that is pushed out of my space releases bound up energy in me — energy for what I'm not quite sure.

I find myself still holding onto outdated ideas. They keep cropping up as I weed out my physical space: "You have a graduate degree, actually three of them! You need to use them." "You're a professional woman by training. You need a white-collar job." And always the underlying, "You gotta be kidding! You can't go a year without regular employment, a steady job."

Each time one of these thoughts pops into my consciousness, I challenge it head on. My degrees don't define me. My quality of life is more important than my past livelihood or identity. I can feel good about myself doing work with my hands. Money comes to me easily and flows through me abundantly.

By the end of the day I have filled two large garbage bags with some of the "excess baggage" I have been carrying around, not just the tangible books and papers, but the more intangible but nonetheless cluttering self-limiting thoughts. I carry them all out to the trash and throw them in, slamming the lid down firmly on them all. I have done battle today with my old self and I have won — at least this round. For today, I am lighter, clearer, more centered and less encumbered than the day before. I stand in front of the "eye of the needle" ready to pass through.

EXERCISE

• JOURNAL

There is a story of a famous rabbi who received many visitors from around the world. One such visitor, noticing the sparseness of the rabbi's house, asked him where his possessions were. The rabbi shot back, "Where are yours?" The visitor, startled, responded, "I'm just visiting." The rabbi replied, "So am I."

What are you holding onto that is not actively giving you energy, that may even be draining it? What is preventing you from letting it go?

• INNER WORK

Meditate on breathing — taking in, letting go...taking in, letting go ...No stops, just a simple, unbroken rhythm.

• EXERCISE

Clean out a closet (or bookcase). Go through it. Give or throw away what no longer "fits."

• YEAR OF JUBILEE COLLAGE

Put up a picture that represents space.

NOTES

WEEK TWO

The strength in me

"Adversity" reveals what is essential — and what is not

Winter landscape
January 18, 1997

There is something so honest about the winter landscape. Naked trees stand, simple and pure, no foliage to fool the eye, their outlines thrust into the unrelenting gray sky. I can make out each limb, each twig, how they grew, how they twist, where they branch out, how they balance one another. I see where a limb has broken, where there is decay, structural weakness, signs of stress or disease. In one piercing glance I can sense a tree's history and predict its future.

Winter, that "in-between" time, between leaf fall and bud burst, is the season to rest, to take stock, to pause. And the tree does it in the open, simply and truthfully, with no artifice or sleight of hand to hide its form. It simply…is.

I know that from a human perspective I would not see a tree as a sentient being, cognizant of its process, yet I admire it all the same. What would it be like to be able to have the grace of that slumbering wood, to stand out open to the universe, visible to all who pass by, with all my faults, all my beauty, all my history, all my hope? What would others see as this "winter" of my own life, this depression, divorce and poor health, stripped of so many "leaves" that have covered my essential form?

EXERCISE

• JOURNAL

Heroism is sometimes defined as an action by an "ordinary" person in response to an extraordinary event. Write about a time in your life when you — in the face of adversity — responded heroically.

• INNER WORK

In prayer or meditation, enter the aloneness of your own being. Experience your own heartbeat, your own body, your own skin. Experience your own sufficiency, your own strength.

• EXERCISE

Pretend you have only an hour to load up what is most important to you in your car. What will you take?

• YEAR OF JUBILEE COLLAGE

Find something that signifies strength.

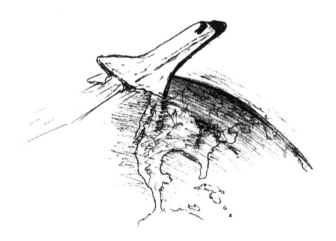

WEEK THREE

Separations

As you break from the old,
move towards the new

D-Day
October 6, 1996

My ex-husband, my younger daughter, Meg, Vilik and I went to Mazzi's for dinner Friday evening, then Meg and I collapsed around ten or so. Saturday we got up early for the hour drive to Eugene; I visited my older daughter, Ann, and Meg took a five-hour Red Cross babysitting class. Ann and I had breakfast and then went to the Saturday market, where I got a large spider plant in a hanging basket, a foxglove to "sacrifice" for the weed collection I'm making for a school assignment, and some garlic basil vinegar.

When Meg and I got back to my place in the late afternoon, Harry came over; he and I went out for coffee to begin talking about divorce proceedings. I've been thinking about it the last few months, as he has, so it seems that the time has come to actually take this final step. Both of us have worked hard to remain friends and family while we separated and through my "coming out" process, integrating my partner into the family and reshaping the whole family structure. It was painfully, frighteningly hard at times, but we did it and came through.

Now it's time for the next step — legally separating assets, dealing with the house, splitting retirement benefits. I hope we can do this gracefully and lovingly as each of our lives continues to change.

It will be both a relief and a challenge for me to take this next step, even though a divorce will mean I need to acquire and pay for my own medical insurance, that I will probably get less of the value of the house than I envisioned, and that our comfortable relationship may change. But it feels clean, honest. I plan to take my own name, my spirit name, as my legal name — no longer Mary Lou, my parents' name for me, or Mrs. Harry N. Chandler, my husband's, or even Mary Chandler, but Mary Heron Dyer.

I am a little scared and a little sad, but ready to step out into this new world I'm about to claim as mine.

We have achieved liftoff!

January 21, 1997

After a busy day that included class, a mammogram, then a trip back to campus for computer lab, I met Harry at the lawyer's office for the third mediation session regarding our divorce. At one point during our session I was convinced we had reached an impasse; I was in tears, just about ready to walk out and hire my own lawyer. But, finally, we reached an agreement. I'll get one payment up front, in two installments: the first will be next month, the second a month after the divorce is finalized. I'll also get 30% of the Public Employees Retirement System money. Most of that will go into investments for retirement, but I'll take out some for the truck and Vilik's dental bills.

It still feels unreal to me that I will actually have money for all those things. The only piece left to do is get a job by June so that I can break even on my monthly expenses — and just enjoy!

It's odd to see myself completely as a separate entity. Today when I got my mammogram I still had Harry's name listed as the primary insuree on my medical card, but it felt like a charade, as though I was masquerading as a married woman. By June I'll be officially divorced, all legal ties cut. It feels clean, honest, more truthful. I'm ready. I feel like the NASA space command at the beginning of a space launch, when the cumbersome, heavy and seemingly earthbound ship breaks its mooring bands and heads toward a distant planet — "We have achieved liftoff!"

EXERCISE

• JOURNAL

Write about a major "leave-taking" of yours. What did it feel like? How did it turn out?

• INNER WORK

In prayer or meditation, create a space around you that is yours alone. It may be helpful to meditate on the seven chakras, or energy points, starting with the first chakra, the base of the spine, site of security and safety, and going up through the other six to the one at the top of the head, the seventh chakra, which attaches us to the source of all. As you claim each chakra for yourself, detach your energy from anyone or anything that is not you.

• EXERCISE

Do something "on your own" this week, something that you would usually do with someone else, like have lunch in a nice restaurant, go for a drive in the country, or maybe repair something by yourself.

• YEAR OF JUBILEE COLLAGE

Draw/find a picture of someone alone and happy, perhaps someone sitting on a park bench, a child playing.

NOTES

WEEK FOUR

New name

It is crucial for us to claim our own power of naming ourselves

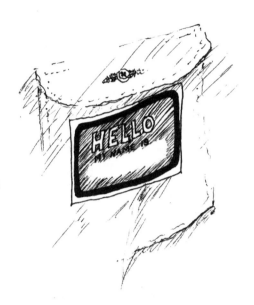

No more a.k.a.
November 2, 1996

Friday was a short school day — a lab had been canceled — so I got to my client's house early. I had to rent a weed whip, including a gas can, so my car still smells like gasoline. I don't think I spilled any, but things like this just keep pushing me into moving toward a truck.

After I got home from pruning and cutting down weeds, I had a message on my answering machine from Sue, who's doing a trade with me: landscaping for graphics. She had prototypes for my business card ready for me to look at; I went right over. The cards look great — four different poses of blue herons to choose from, plus 24 different type settings.

I took them home to look over. When I looked at my new name, one that I plan to make officially mine when the divorce is finalized, I felt sad and lonely, like a cold wind was blowing through my soul. It brought up feelings of isolation, thoughts of death. My dreams that night were of letting go of Harry, of my garden going dormant, of pulling up dying plants, of getting ready for the winter. This is also a weekend my partner and I are spending apart, by mutual consent — a time apart that includes no phone contact, so I have lots of time to sit with my feelings.

Theoretically, I understand what's going on in me. Carol Gilligan, in her landmark book, *In A Different Voice,*[2] challenged the male-only model of development theory that claimed the stages of all human growth go from identity to intimacy. She posited, and to my mind, using my own life as a measure, successfully proves, that women have this order reversed. Due to early socialization, sex-role conditioning, and being raised, on the whole, by other females, we go way into adulthood in an unbroken line, putting intimacy, relationship with others, before our own identity. We get to this second stage of claiming our identity, if we get there at all, much later than men, whose adult task is to be able to find intimacy.

According to Gilligan's theory, I'm right on target. Theory, however, is cold comfort right now. I'm lonely. I've been connected to Harry since I was 18 years old; I met him on my first day of independence from my parents, on the first job I ever had. I've felt comfortable with his last name all these years, even during our ten-year separation.

Now, for better or worse, it's time to step out, step away, step into my own being, my own identity. I know that, in my very bones...but today there's a cold wind blowing at the door.

EXERCISE

• JOURNAL

In the movie, "Shirley Valentine, " Shirley says,

I've led such a little life and even that'll be over pretty soon. I've allowed myself to lead this little life when inside me there's so much more and it's all gone unused and now it will never be. Why do we get all this life if we don't ever use it? That's why Shirley Valentine disappeared. She got lost in all this unused life.

What kinds of little lives are we allowing ourselves to live? When does it become too late?

She finally says, "I used to be the mother. I used to be the wife, but now I'm Shirley Valentine." Is there any way of keeping one's own identity while also taking on the roles of wife and mother? [Or any other role that may infringe on our own sense of self?] What would make it easier?

• INNER WORK

Mary Daly, a famous feminist theologian, in her keystone book, *Beyond God the Father,* claims that women have had the power of naming taken from us. She goes further to claim that "...to exist humanly is to name the self, the world, and God."[3] In prayer or meditation, invoke your spirit self to come to you. What does she call you? What is your "spirit" name?

• EXERCISE

Meet and talk with someone new this week. Reveal yourself without stating whether or not you are in a relationship, whether or not you have children.

• YEAR OF JUBILEE COLLAGE

Put your spirit name on your collage.

CHAPTER NINE ENDNOTES

1.   Heinrich, Bernd. *A Year in the Maine Wood.* Addison-Wesley Publication Co.: Reading, MA, 1994.

2.   Gilligan, Carol. *In a Different Voice: Psychological Theory and Women's Development.* Cambridge: Harvard University Press, 1982.

3.   Daly, Mary. *Beyond God the Father: Toward a Philosophy of Women's Liberation.* Boston: Beacon Press, 1973.

X

Self-Sufficiency

**True Masters are those who have chosen to make a life,
rather than a living.**

— Neale Donald Walsch

Introduction

*J*did something very special for my fortieth birthday — I purchased a car, the first one I had ever had in my own name. At the time I was still married, with three children at home, yet somehow this car came to mean more to me than just a way to get from point A to point B. It ended up taking me into my new life, to a place I never even imagined existed.

Somehow I knew that that little red Toyota Tercel was my own "time transport" to another reality, far from the one I had embraced until that point. So I also knew my new car had to have a name befitting its momentous destiny. I chewed on it for awhile, then settled for "Arachne," the Greek word for "spider." An odd name for a car, I suppose, until we get to the meaning. Another name for spider is "spinster," "one who spins." A secondary meaning is, of course, more familiar, a woman never married.

Now that obviously did not apply to me — I married when I was scarcely twenty. I never did have a chance to try my wings as a single adult, slipping from family home into marriage with nary a spare moment to imagine myself standing alone in the world.

Yet the "spinster," before it took on the negative connotations of undesirable and unworthy-for-matrimony single woman, was someone who, like the spider for whom I named my car, was able to "spin" out of herself, out of her brain and heart and hands, what she needed to maintain herself and provide for her needs.

Some who read this book may be in a permanent relationship, others in between, others, by choice or fate, alone. Yet I think Arachne, the spinner, has much to teach us all. We ourselves, from our deepest place, must shape and weave our own lives into a beautiful pattern. Our lives are, hopefully, filled with family and friends, with a sense of belonging and safety in the larger world. Yet there is no one, no one at all, who can — or should — take the shuttle of our lives and weave it for us. For creating the pattern of our own lives is our greatest responsibility — and our greatest gift.

WEEK ONE

Who are you?

You have within yourself all you need to succeed

Hestia

November 20, 1996

Yesterday, while I was shopping at the co-op for a new blank journal, I found a greeting card with a picture that touched me. The front shows a small clearing surrounded by the trunks of large trees. In the midst of the clearing a circle of stones surrounds a young woman with long hair who kneels, unclothed, reaching down toward a small evergreen plant growing beside her in the circle. Her face is pensive. Yet somehow, from nothing except her own inner light, she is nourishing the life, the promise, of the small seedling. When I look at her I see a young Hestia, guardian of her own hearth.

This young Hestia's body, free of clothing, strikes a chord in me. It brings to mind the story of St. Francis of Assisi, who became a mendicant in thirteenth century medieval Italy. He turned away publicly from his former life, stripping himself bare and handing his cloth merchant father the beautiful clothes that had been his. Then he walked away, naked, trusting solely in the providence of God.

I, too, am emptying out my own life, stripping myself bare of who I thought I was. Like St Francis, I have left my past behind. Like Hestia, it is up to me to nourish my own hearth. I ponder the picture of this crouching young woman, who seems to have nothing but is aglow with promise, and I know that as I trust in myself and the abundance of the universe, I, too, will be able to "grow my own life."

Self-employed
May 3, 1996

"I was thinking around six or eight dollars an hour. I can start Tuesday. I'll be here around seven." That was fast. The ink was hardly dry on my unemployment application and I was already contracting for my first yardwork job. My first client, a friend from Unity, and I had just toured her yard. I listened to myself saying things like, "It looks like your grass in the front lawn is gone. Too much shade. You'll at least have to reseed, if not totally resod, and make sure you get a mix of grass seed that does better in the shade," and "I think a trellis right in front of this west-facing window would give you some fast shade with a clematis or passion flower."

How different from a little over a week ago, when I was working at a rape and domestic violence agency where my comments ran more along the lines of, "Are you safe now?" "When is the abuser coming home?" "Let me tell you about our confidential shelter." Somehow sick lawns have so much more appeal to me in this moment than people in crisis. As the T-shirt proclaims, "Been there. Done that. Have the T-shirt."

Jubilant, I drove home, icicles from the surprise mid-spring hailstorm still melting in my hair. No desk job, this. Hard physical labor, selling myself, learning fast, pacing this 50-year-old body whose most recent job was simply to house my brain. Is this whole enterprise crazy? Can I pull it off, or should I be sending resumés to other agencies, looking for another counseling job with high stress and mediocre pay?

As I sit on my bed tonight, writing this page before I go to sleep, I glance across at my altar where a card proclaims, "If you don't run your own life, someone else will!" I'm glad it will be one of the last things I see before I close this journal and turn out the light, which I must do soon. The sun is coming up early tomorrow, and there are gardens waiting.

I get paid for this?!
August 7, 1996

I was at the farmer's market when it opened this morning; I needed to buy plants for one of my clients' garden. Wandering through the stalls I found canna lilies, lacecap hydrangeas, oxalys, hollyhock, althea rose, butterfly bush, bush impatiens, yarrow, hardy fuchsia, gooseneck lysimachia, crocosmia and Japanese fern. The car ended up so filled with plants I had to make two trips. Later in the morning my client and I went to Garland's Nursery together to make more selections. We quickly zeroed in on another lacecap hydrangea, three azaleas, a mountain laurel and a dwarf juniper.

I was "on the clock" for six hours today   — getting paid for shopping for plants, networking with growers, and generally having the time of my life.

Later in the afternoon I was home in time for my soap opera, then read the paper and napped until the day had cooled. Out in my own garden in the early evening, I saw that part of my potato plants were dying down. I knelt next to the seed bed and thrust my hands into the soil to harvest the first of the potato crop. It was like a treasure hunt, not knowing where or how many potatoes I would find in the rich, black soil. Finally I had a gallon container filled with potatoes of different hues — white, yellow, red, purple.

Potatoes are deceptive. They're most productive and ready to harvest when, to the naked eye, the plant looks dead above ground. It's a reminder to me — sometimes it's necessary to go below the surface appearance, to get on my knees and get my hands dirty digging, to find the treasures hidden deep in the ground. Over three months into my Year of Jubilee, I have found that the deeper I dig into the soil around my own life, the more I find it will nourish me through the "winter" of what on paper looks like underemployment. I am learning more about my joy, about what really nurtures me, and learning how I can get others to pay me to follow the stirring of my heart.

Not another referral!
June 9, 1996

Always prompt to pay me, one of my clients slipped an envelope with my weekly paycheck into my hand at the church potluck. Along with the check was someone's business card, across which she had printed in small letters, "Mary, call her. She's a super lady and needs help with general gardening and stinging nettles down by the creek."

I couldn't help but groan. This was my fourth referral from her — and I haven't called any of them. I'm up to twenty hours a week just with her, and there's lots more to do at her place this summer. I've begun to lay out a pathway, from scratch — so far I've dug up the sod and filled the area in with two cubic yards of sand. I still have to remove the aggregate tiles, water the sand, level it off, smooth it out, rent a manual tamper, replace the tiles in their permanent location, fill in around them with soil, plant moss, Corsican mint or thyme between them, level the remaining yard, smooth out the new topsoil, seed it with a grass mix and crocus bulbs, plant a circle of shade-lovers under the maple, water the seed...

So, what will I do with this deluge of people, this flood of possibilities? My life is indeed "filling up and spilling over" with the abundance of the universe. And to think I was worried about not having enough work....

EXERCISE

• JOURNAL

Brainstorm as fast as you can, completing the following sentence 30 times. "I can...."

• INNER WORK

In prayer or meditation, see the whole world contained with all that is needed. Everything comes with its potential already embedded in its genetic code. Pick a seed and watch it break open and grow to its full promise.

• EXERCISE

Call someone who is self-employed, who has created their own work life. Have coffee with them. Pick their brain.

• YEAR OF JUBILEE COLLAGE

Sit down for fifteen minutes and make something out of something you have on hand.

NOTES

WEEK TWO

A picture emerges

You can weave all the strands of
your life into a perfect whole

Weave, weave

May 30, 1996

"Hi. I'm Mary Chandler. I'm a Master Gardener...." I paused for a moment to wait for the laughter to subside. After all, I was at a workshop for helping professionals entitled, "Promoting a Fighting Spirit: Helping People Cope with Cancer." I then continued, "I also have a master's in counseling, and I used to do a lot of hospital and bereavement work. I'm going to begin co-facilitating a bereavement support group in Corvallis next month."

As we went around the room and introduced ourselves, other people's lives seemed so tidy, so all-of-one-piece. "I'm Ann, a social worker at Emanuel," or "I'm Lynn; I work with oncology outpatients." Each statement seemed to strike only one note.

I have danced to so many tunes in my own life. I've been an English literature buff, housewife/mother, pastoral theologian and parish worker, volunteer coordinator at a domestic violence agency and, most recently, Master Gardener. And now I've been accepted into the horticultural program at the local community college. What harmonies, what melodies, I wonder, will emerge during this Year of Jubilee? If I could actually see these different parts of my life, if they had shape and color and texture, how would I weave them together?

I scrutinize the different strands of my life, holding them up to the light to see which ones still let joy shine through. Catholic/Lutheran theologian? No. That strand goes on the discard pile. But spirituality itself? A resounding yes. I'll keep this strand and weave it into a new pattern. Domestic violence agency work? A definitive no. But counseling itself? Yes. But with what clients? Maybe people with life-threatening illness, or their survivors? Don't know yet. Writing? A loud yes. I try to picture my life a year from now. How exactly is it I plan to make a living? Doodling, I start to draw a business card.

I imagine it slate gray, a blue heron outlined on it. Through the middle I jot my name, not my legal name, but my spirit name: *Mary Heron Dyer*. OK, now what? Oh yes, degrees. Well, the master's in English literature doesn't count for much. How about my master's in scripture and theology? I jot down an "M.A." after my name. Then of course my "M.S." in counseling. That will be useful. Plus "N.C.C." (Nationally Certified Counselor). That will come in handy. And "Master Gardener," important to me but probably few others. Maybe I'll have to have a two-sided business card by next summer, along with a gardening motif.

Then what? Oh, yes, specialties. "Domestic violence/sexual assault/incest survivors"? I have credentials and experience, but no. Not again. How about "Spirituality"? Great. "Bereavement"? Don't know yet, so I settle on "transitions." I certainly have first-hand experience of that.

"Groups"? I'm open to that. "Couples/families"? No. "Individuals." Yes.

O.K. It's taking shape: Don't quite have my state license yet, although it isn't yet required in Oregon. Don't want to mess with third-party payments. So how about $25-65 sliding scale? This weaving is turning into a tapestry. Oh yes, better add my phone number. I don't need a second business-only line at this point. A beautiful counseling space I will affirm will open
up by winter. And so it is.

EXERCISE

• JOURNAL

If something happened right now to cut off your source of income, what would you do? Jot down some ideas — don't limit yourself. Be creative and open, the only limitation is that you must think you would enjoy it.

• INNER WORK

In prayer or meditation, picture your own life unfolding. First a single-cell inside your mother's womb, then a baby, a child on a bike, going to school, leaving home, then up to the present. Feel the joy of gaining coordination and mobility, of mastering simple tasks, of learning how to take care of yourself.

• EXERCISE

Design a business card.

• YEAR OF JUBILEE COLLAGE

Put the card on your collage.

NOTES

WEEK THREE

Money and financial security

Be creative and think big about income, investments and opportunities

"Argue for your limits, and sure enough, they're yours"
May 23, 1996

The title of this entry popped into my mind yesterday, as I was mulling over (euphemism for "worrying to death") my financial situation. It's a quote from Richard Bach's book, *Illusions: The Adventures of a Reluctant Messiah*[1]. It's so easy to reduce myself to counting pennies, measuring teaspoons, weighing out my life in "coffee spoons", like J. Alfred Prufrock in T. S. Eliot's poem of the same name. I find myself counting my financial "coffee spoons" over and over again in my mind. "If I manage to get a $4,000 student loan, plus $250 a month grading, plus 20 hours a week at $6.00 work-study, I'll be just a little worse off this time next year and then I can maintain a very moderate lifestyle until retirement."

But nature herself is prodigal, one packet of carrot seeds enough to fill a whole garden. The rule of nature is profligacy, abundance. I need to remember that. The time has come to throw the coffee spoon away — to dream dreams that cannot be contained, dreams that spill out and over, that sprout and grow into the rich, ripe garden of my life.

In the zone
October 4, 1996

It's Friday again. This week of school went faster and easier, possibly because I actually relaxed and let it happen. I tried to stay in the present, not worrying about the next day, the next task, not trying to get everything done perfectly, with the "t's" crossed and the "i's" dotted, but just maintained a basic understanding of the material involved in the classwork.

Usually I'm intense and competitive, pushing myself to the limit. Today, for instance, I had decided my "success" point was going to be five hours of work. But the rain got progressively worse, and, finally, drenched, my hair flattened and wet, my glasses steamy and muddy, I told Sue I'd had it for the day and was going home to take a hot bath, even if it only had been three hours. "Giving up" felt like a greater success than slipping around the clay slope in the rain for another self-imposed two hours.

What would those additional two hours have proved? That I could do it? That I was tough? That I could compete with any guy? That I literally didn't know when to come in out of the rain? Leaving proved so much more. That I could allow myself a little luxury on a rainy day. That it wasn't that important that I earn that extra twenty bucks. And, most importantly, that I trust that the universe will provide for me if I just get out of my own way and let it.

A CD doesn't always play music
January 9, 1997

I recently had my hair cut at a salon owned and run by a young couple "savvy" about finances, already planning their retirement. Stephen asked me what I was getting people for Christmas. Then he told me he and his wife were giving each other CD's. Surprised, I responded, "Compact disks?"

"No. Certificates of Deposit for our retirement."

I've just turned 51; I have no investments. It's time to figure out this part of my life. Until ten years ago I was in a traditional marriage, my financial future tied to my husband's. We had our own house but never money to invest for our future;

our three children managed to gobble up any excess. We counted on social security and a public employees' retirement fund to get us through our "golden years." Even after we separated I assumed the same plan held; I would get a legal divorce when he retired and split the assets.

When he decided last fall to finalize our separation and file for divorce, it disrupted my spurious sense of security. But as the divorce proceedings progressed I learned that, in addition to the money I am due for my share of the home we owned together, I will have immediate access to my part of the retirement funds when the divorce is final.

This unexpected windfall, although it still feels like "play" money, calls for a new step in my ability to think. I talked to an investor friend; soon we were discussing mutual funds, rollovers, broker fees, bears and bulls.

It's exciting and a little scary to think I'll actually have real investment capital after the divorce. I want to invest this money wisely. Can I?

EXERCISE

• JOURNAL

What are your underlying beliefs about money? Is there enough? What is enough? Is it within your power to create what you need or do you always have to "think small?"

• INNER WORK

In prayer or meditation, reflect on the following saying of Jesus:

Think of the flowers growing in the fields; they never have to work or spin; yet I assure you that not even Solomon in all his regalia was robed like one of these. Now if that is how God clothes the grass in the field which is there today and thrown into the furnace tomorrow, will God not much more look after you...

(Matthew 6:28-30)

• EXERCISE

Face your biggest fear, e.g., "I will be a bag lady." Challenge it. Invent one sentence which challenges it, a truth that is in the present tense and is not limiting. Act as if it is real. Claim it. Repeat it, scream it, sing it, make it your own.[2]

• YEAR OF JUBILEE COLLAGE

Put a card with your "mantra" on it about the abundance of the universe.

WEEK FOUR

Connecting to center

Abundance flows

"The floodgates of heaven..."
Part I
August 14, 1996

Yesterday evening my partner and I went grocery shopping at the local co-op, where she spotted a beautiful Guatemalan bag. I was torn between wanting to buy it for her as a gift and feeling financially "tight", wondering when my application for a student loan would be processed. Yet I wanted to trust that my new belief about the abundance of the universe was true.

It reminded me of a passage from the Old Testament prophet Micah, who speaks of the demand of tithing prescribed to the Hebrew people.

Bring the full tithes and dues to the storehouse so that there may be food in my house, and then see if I do not open the floodgates of heaven for you and pour out blessing for you in abundance. (Micah 3:6-12)

How striking that the floodgates of heaven do not come until the people, in good faith, have already given. Generosity and trusting in providence are the first steps toward prosperity.

After wandering around the store for a few minutes I came back, picked up the bag and bought it. It gave me great pleasure to give it to my partner. I am learning to flow more easily and give more freely. As my heart continues to open, so will the floodgates of heaven.

"The floodgates of heaven..."
Part II
August 15, 1996

It's been a challenging process not to have a regular paycheck these past few months, not to know what my income is going to be. It's tempting to hoard, to play the cards close to my chest, to guard my assets and protect my interests. Yet the whole point of this Year of Jubilee is to let go — of negativity, of limitation, of any way of thinking, feeling or being that stands in the way of my living completely and confidently in the present.

That point was sorely tested this week. I had anticipated $4,000 in financial aid for school, but was awarded only $1,500. The financial aid office claimed they never got my application, and based the amount on higher earnings than I had actually made in the past year. I was stunned; I was furious. This school has, time and time again, screwed up, lost things, misinterpreted them, given me inaccurate or incomplete information.

After my rage abated, I started brainstorming. Could I refinance my truck? Could I go to a loan officer at the local bank about a student loan?

The latter seemed like a good idea; I headed down to the bank to talk with a loan officer. There I learned I am actually eligible for $6,700 in loans, rather than the original $4,000 I initially thought. In one short day I had lost $4,000 — then gained it back, along with another $2,700.

When I was angry the energy stopped flowing through me. The money stopped flowing to me. As I let go and affirmed that the universe was, indeed, abundant, the money flowed to me easily and more prolifically than even I had envisioned.

EXERCISE

• JOURNAL

In the past week you were to create a powerful one-sentence statement about abundance. As you practiced it, what happened?

• INNER WORK

In prayer or meditation, picture money as energy flowing to you and from you. It is not static, it does not have to be "saved," but it simply comes, as currency, running through your life. It comes easily and abundantly, there is always enough, there is no need to worry about tomorrow. All is being provided.

• EXERCISE

Give some currency away this week. It could be money, time for a friend, sharing expertise with someone who needs your skills, a check to a cause you believe in but never got around to giving money to. Be aware that you are generous, that the more you give, the more you are open to receiving.

• YEAR OF JUBILEE COLLAGE

Find/draw a picture of something that represents abundance to you.

CHAPTER TEN ENDNOTES

1.   Bach, Richard. *Illusions: The Adventures of a Reluctant Messiah.* NY: Delacorte Press, 1977.

2.   Idea taken from Suzie Orman's *The 9 Steps to Financial Freedom.* NY: Crown Publishers, 1997.

NOTES

XI

Burning Through

Time and trouble will tame an advanced young woman,
but an advanced old woman is uncontrollable by any force.

—Dorothy Sayers

Introduction

*T*here are many theories flying around about whether or not we choose to be born into a particular family, culture, nation. They range from the pure random chance model to the pre-knowledge of a soul waiting for the perfect place to incarnate, and I have at various times in my life found myself arguing for both sides of this conundrum. But in a sense this first birth, into physical reality, isn't really as important as the second birth — the birthing of our deepest selves that is the work each of us is given.

Adrienne Rich, in her poem, "What is Possible,"[1] says that

If the mind were clear
and if the mind were simple you could take this mind
this particular state and say
'This is how I would live if I could choose:
this is what is possible....'
But the mind
of the woman imagining all this the mind
that allows all this to be possible
Does not so easily work free from remorse....

And yet can you imagine a world where you are indeed "free from remorse", a world where your own birthing is the most compelling mission you could desire? Too selfish perhaps? Too much guilt? Too many pressures and expectations from other people? Wendy Martin, author of *An American Triptych: Anne Bradshaw, Emily Dickinson, Adrienne Rich*, claims that: "...women have a mission to survive...and to be whole people...this can save the world." She goes further, stating that "we have to save the world by doing it for ourselves — for all women."[2]

Lastly, a word from Isak Dinesen, author of *Out of Africa*:

Women, when they are old enough to have done with the business of being women, and can let loose their strength, must be the most powerful creatures in the world.[3]

So now it is time — time to be strong, to claim your own uniqueness, to save the world not by losing yourself but by becoming yourself — burning away all that is not of worth to you, burning through to your own power and beauty.

WEEK ONE

Crashing or creating?

New life can come from the ashes of the old

Burning out or burning through?
July 15, 1996

I finished the tree house this week; it's wonderful. Yesterday I was one of the few Master Gardener volunteers available to spend the morning at the impossibly busy Extension Office and field questions from home gardeners. The desk was piled high with unfinished requests for information and bagged plant and bug samples; I put down my unread paper and dug in. "Why is my zucchini growing to four inches, then rotting on the end?" Answer: Until both female and male flowers are in bloom at the same time, they aren't pollinated and cannot grow further and will just rot. "What do you recommend for cover crops?" Answer: hairy vetch, annual rye and crimson clover. "Is a three-year rotation sufficient for vegetables?" Yes, but four would be even better. "Can I solarize young blueberry plants?" No, it will harm the roots. "Can I make wine from an unknown variety plum tree?" Probably, but no guarantees. By noon I had logged in over twenty completed responses, three times my average.

In the afternoon I drove to McMinnville to see my daughter. The day was warm, in the mid-80's, refreshing after the last week's heat wave. I put Scott Joplin on the tape-player and turned up the sound as high as my ears could stand. The sweet smell of hay being harvested permeated the air as I passed fields where the young corn was almost waist high, saw young colts frolicking in the pastures, watched blackbirds chase crows in the bright blue sky. All my senses were alive; I was fully present in my own life. I started crying, the joy pouring out in my tears because I couldn't hold any more.

As I returned to Corvallis later that evening, I heard the voice of my friend "Mary also" (so named because we used to facilitate groups together; to make it easier for everyone, I was "Mary" and she became "Mary also") . "I guess you just burned out." She was trying to figure out why I had changed so much at the domestic violence agency, and been so unhappy there the last few months. But I really didn't burn out. I burned through.

I burned away what wasn't important any longer and burned through to my own sense of self. It is a self apart from a title, from a position of responsibility, from moving faster and faster just to stay in place. I burned through — to my own joy, my own peace, my own rhythms, my own self-sufficiency. And that is beginning to make all the difference.

EXERCISE

• JOURNAL

Write about a time when you "crashed and burned." What was on the other side?

• INNER WORK

In prayer or meditation, fashion a pot out of clay, shape it, color it. Put it in a kiln to burn off its impurities.

• EXERCISE

Pick something this week, large or small, that is no longer "you." Perhaps it is a committee you don't really want to be on anymore, an obligation that feels onerous. Let it go.

• YEAR OF JUBILEE COLLAGE

Find/draw a picture of fire and put it on your board.

NOTES

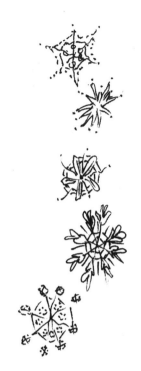

WEEK TWO

New self-images

Each of us is totally unique and beautiful

You learn fast for a girl!

June 17, 1996

Michael, my landscaping companion, and I spent today together, putting posts into holes, nailing 2x4 braces, measuring and cutting crossbars. In between our tasks we managed little snippets of conversation, exchanging our life stories in one- or two-sentence "sound bytes."

It's been awhile since I've worked side by side with a man in a commonly regarded male domain; it brings up lots of early childhood memories. I was a tomboy from the moment I could pull myself up on my baby feet. I climbed trees, rode bikes, wrestled, and played football with the neighborhood boys (until my mother made me give it up when I started high school). I would get into rock fights with boys and catch their hurled rocks with my bare hands. I loved being active, physical, competitive.

Now there's some good-natured banter as Michael and I learn to work together. I told him today that his only advantages in this job are the ease with which he can pee without inside plumbing and the freedom with which he can peel off his shirt in the heat.

At noon, replete in brimmed hat, flannel shirt and kneepads, I made a run to the local hardware store. As I strode in, I waved off help. ("No," I tried to say with

my body language, "I know exactly what I'm doing and what I want. I belong here!")
After I got a pound of nails, I marched up to the counter, proclaiming, "I also need a
Swanson Speed Square." "No," I wave off another brand name, "I want the best. I
want a Swanson, not a Stanley."

I returned, triumphant, to my new world of wood shavings and circular saws.
"Look, Michael," I proclaimed, holding up my carpenter's square, "I got one too!"
The work went faster with each of us having a hammer, pencil, tape measure, nails
and, of course, our own Swanson Speed Square (which I hadn't even heard of before
this morning).

I got into the rhythm of hammering metal supports for the 2x4's onto the
4x4 posts, matching Michael nail for nail, blow for blow, measuring crisply and accurately and proudly. "Hey", I found myself muttering under my breath, "I can do this
professionally. Just watch me!"

And Michael did, taking his measure of me in his own quiet way. I must have
passed inspection for, at the end of the day, he told me, "You learn fast for a girl."

"When I am an old lady, I shall wear purple..."
July 16, 1996

Yesterday was so hot Vilik and I had to find an air-conditioned restaurant and
movie to hide out in as soon as I got home from work. When we got out of the movie
at nine, the evening had cooled off enough for me to want to go home, but the mall
was right across from the theater and she still wanted to roam around.

I was too tired to go into the store; it was too hot to sit in the car. So I took
out the chaise lounge I had in the back, opened it and set it up in front of the car on
the sidewalk. I lay back, relaxing, enjoying the hint of a breeze that caressed my face.
It was an interesting experience to so obviously not go along with the "normal"
behaviors of people at a shopping mall.

People on the way to their cars stopped when I smiled, and we talked about
the weather. Later, as the lights went on at dusk, I sought out a more solitary space
under a tree and watched the clear sky turn silky black, the last vestiges of pink
sneaking away over the sharply etched mountains in the west.

And I reflected on how hard it was to do something as harmless and just possibly borderline eccentric as sitting in a chaise lounge in a parking lot. I had never seen anyone else do it.

But I am reminded of that beautiful poem which begins, "When I am an old lady I shall wear purple." Life is too short to let my projection of strangers' thoughts keep me in the artificially narrow and rigidly enforced confines of "acceptable" behavior.

So, here I come, world. I'm wearing purple and carrying a lawn chair. Move over!

EXERCISE

• JOURNAL

Make a list of those things which are special or distinct about you.

• INNER WORK

In prayer or meditation, picture the whole universe, with all its myriads of solar systems, of stars so distant it takes thousands of light years for their light to reach the earth. Then slowly bring your focus back to this planet, this country, this state, this town, this street, to your very own self. Feel yourself the center, the absolute loving, creative, unique center, of this entire universe, and give thanks.

• EXERCISE

Do something "eccentric" in the next week, something that reveals or reinforces your own uniqueness.

• YEAR OF JUBILEE COLLAGE

Put a memento of this week on your board to remind yourself of your own uniqueness.

WEEK THREE

Satisfaction from within

You have everything you need to succeed inside yourself

Generic honey
June 5, 1996

Summer's almost here; it's warm enough to sit out in the patio of one of my favorite restaurants again. Bricks cover the ground inside the large, fenced space; nooks and crannies offer privacy. In the center of the patio grows a beautiful old apple tree, its small green fruits not yet a danger to unwary diners' heads.

I sought out an arbor-shaded corner where I sat, solitary, watching the water spots my glass left on the rustic picnic table. Then I heard a buzzing nearby, a honeybee, gathering nectar from the beautiful but unrecognizable plant whose boughs interlaced across the trellis over my head, providing a natural canopy of leaves through which dapples of westerly sun lightly danced. Clusters of five-petalled white flowers hung down, piquing my horticultural curiosity. A waiter informed me it was a kiwi vine, which I already knew as a relatively new and very successful commercial crop in the Willamette Valley of Oregon.

People came and went. I recognized some — a volunteer from my former agency; the head of Women's Studies at OSU where I taught a film class several summers ago; an emergency department physician from the local hospital; a couple of men looking suspiciously like Catholic priests in lay clothes.

As I people-watched, I reflected that it still seems a little strange, not setting my sights on becoming one defining thing — political activist, teacher, minister, social service worker, although there's a little bit of each in me.

But I was content, off in my secret corner. The honeybee overhead had gathered nectar from many different kinds of flowers, and so had I. Perhaps I can't put a clear sign on myself like "Clover Honey" or "Apple Honey," but mine is all the sweeter because it has a touch, a hint, a taste, of all the places I have been.

From banquet to bouquet
May 28, 1996

A beautiful, delightfully slow day at the coast. Vilik and I came down here several days ago. There are no watches, no time schedules, nothing that "has" to be done. This morning I was up around nine, late for me, then strolled to my favorite cafe in Newport for coffee, breakfast roll and leisurely reading of the morning paper, capped off by the crossword puzzle.

As I wandered back to the cabin, I stopped here and there, creating a bouquet of flowers I found growing wild alongside the road or in untended vacant lots.

By the time I got back to the cabin, I had a handful of nature's bounty — purple clover, hairy vetch, with its small purple peapod flowers, bright orange California poppies, yellow buttercups, a white morning glory, pink thrift, white candytuft, and three wild roses — white, pink and plum. I arranged them in a clear kitchen drinking glass where they will spend the day brightening our small wooden dining room table.

By midafternoon we were ready to run a few errands, but it wasn't until we got to the bank to deposit some money that my partner asked me the date. I paused for a moment, my mind still adjusted to "vacation time," before it finally came to me. "May 28," I replied.

Then it hit me. It was the day of the annual volunteer appreciation dessert, an event that, when I was an agency employee, had consumed me in its preparation and then would have occupied me all day and well into the evening. Even after I was fired, the executive director asked me if I would be willing to attend so that the volunteers could honor me and have "closure." I declined, not wanting to go on with the company "lie" that I had just decided suddenly to move on. I also declined, I think, because I am coming to a deeper and deeper understanding that praise, and blame, for that matter, are, at the deepest level, irrelevant if not entrapping. Praise and blame put the focus on doing, not being, and the judgment of the quality of that "doing" on other people.

There is something so real, so true, about these flowers at my side as I write this, so true about me, who saw and appreciated their gift, that all the banquets in the world pale in comparison.

EXERCISE

• JOURNAL

Write down some things that give you satisfaction about yourself, little things, things that would not appear on a traditional resumé.

• INNER WORK

In prayer or meditation, reflect on this saying: "Don't just do something. Sit there." Let go of your list of accomplishments, your desire to "do" something meaningful or valued in the world. Simply sit and appreciate your own beingness, your own spirit.

• EXERCISE

Do something this week that no one else knows about, that you take pleasure in. It can be just for you or some "random act or kindness or senseless beauty."

• YEAR OF JUBILEE COLLAGE

Place a representation on the board of something that you value about yourself.

NOTES

WEEK FOUR

Integration

All that you have, all that you are,
makes one perfect whole

"The Chambered Nautilus"
May 19, 1996

Tonight I went to a concert given by Jubilate, a women's choir. In the audience and on stage I kept seeing people I had known through my connection with domestic violence work, my former life. The woman acting as usher was also the board chairperson of the agency that fired me; she had not only jumped on the band-wagon of my firing but had built and driven it. I managed to slide by her, avoiding eye contact, resenting it when she greeted my partner as if nothing had happened. But after I slid into my seat, thinking I had eluded her, I looked up onto the stage to see her outline grotesquely magnified and projected, larger than life, onto the curtains. It reminded me of how we can project our fears and make them into shadowy monsters looming in our path, but it also reminded me that we are the ones, ultimately, who do the projecting. I felt conflicting emotions, as fleeting as the shadows thrown onto the stage by the lighting. Hope, joy, sadness, uncertainty, even a sense of enlightenment, followed quickly by confusion.

The songs were beautiful, energizing, compelling. They contained the distillation of all that is true and pure in each of us, that god/dess self that holds us all in unity deeper than our surface divisions. Carried on the wings of the music, I realized that I cannot simply discard my past and toss it aside, glorious in my new skin, my new shell, my new garment. Feminist, political activist, lesbian, worker in the domestic violence movement — I am still all those things. But brushing up against my so-recent past showed me I don't understand how I am still connected and how I need to grow beyond those definitions.

Then I called to mind the chambered nautilus, and it suddenly seemed a fitting symbol. This nautilus, Greek for "sailor," is a beautiful mollusk whose shell in cross section reveals a spiral, the ever-growing segments each sealed off from its former home, now grown too snug for the expanding animal. Each time it leaves its former home it secretes a hard pearly substance over its mouth, leaving only a small hole in the middle of the now empty chamber to allow for either water or air as ballast as it travels the open seas. When it wants to float on the ocean waves, it expels the water from the innermost chambers; when it wants to dive deep, it floods them with salt water, taking itself to the very depths.

Oliver Wendell Holmes, a famous nineteenth-century New England poet, wrote of this process of the chambered nautilus, in a poem of the same name:

> *Year after year beheld the silent toil*
> *That spread his lustrous coil;*
> *Still, as the spiral grew,*
> *He left the past year's dwelling for the new,*
> *Stole with soft step its shining archway through,*
> *Built up its idle door,*
> *Stretched in his last-found home, and knew the old no more.*

He ends with these still prophetic lines:

> *Build thee more stately mansions, O my soul,*
> *As the swift seasons roll!*
> *Leave thy low-vaulted past!*
> *Let each new temple, nobler than the last,*
> *Shut thee from heaven with a dome more vast,*
> *Till thou at length art free,*
> *Leaving thine outgrown shell by life's unresting sea!*[4]

I am a fellow traveler with my distant cousin, the chambered nautilus, far from my familiar shore, but I am still all that I was and will become — and it is all one, all whole. I carry it all deep inside me as I spiral beyond each set of self-imposed limits.

EXERCISE

• JOURNAL

Make a list of all the different kinds of activities, hobbies, jobs, lives you have had so far.

• INNER WORK

In prayer or meditation, picture yourself as a baby, then a young child. Follow your life up to the present, then far into the future — to death and beyond. Feel yourself a complete whole, pulling together all parts of your life.

• EXERCISE

Take something from your past, something that no longer seems to "fit," and find the blessing in it. What did you learn? How did it change you? How is it continuing to affect you now?

• YEAR OF JUBILEE COLLAGE

Find/draw a picture of a metamorphosis (e.g., caterpillar to butterfly, seed to tree). Place it on your board.

CHAPTER ELEVEN ENDNOTES

1.   Rich, Adrienne. "What is Possible," from *A Wild Patience Has Taken Me This Far: Poems 1978-1981*. W. W. Norton & Co.: NY, 1986.

2.   Martin, Wendy. *An American Triptych: Anne Bradshaw, Emily Dickinson, Adrienne Rich*. Chapel Hill: University of North Carolina Press, 1986.

3.   Dinesen, Isak. "The Monkey," from *Seven Gothic Tales*. NY: Vintage Books, 1972.

4.   Holmes, Oliver Wendell. "The Chambered Nautilus," from *The Complete Poems of Oliver Wendell Holmes*. Houghton Mifflin Co.: NY, 1927.

NOTES

XII

The sheer inevitability of wings

*Do you remember
what happens
inside a cocoon?*

You liquefy...

You melt...

*Congealing
in impossible darkness
the sheer
inevitability
of wings.*

—Kim Rosen

Introduction

I laughed out loud when I came across a description of aphids as "crawlers and reluctant flyers." I pictured these soft-bodied little green garden pests hanging onto that last piece of leaf as they were being stalked by a predator. Instead of trusting the wings they grew in adulthood, they crawl along, terrorized (well, maybe I'm anthropomorphizing a bit), waiting to become another insect's meal. There they sit, those minute pieces of living matter, in their little world of cabbage leaves and rosebuds, not daring to imagine anything greater.

The phrase "crawlers and reluctant flyers" tickles my funny bone. I understand the aphids' predicament. At times I too am a "crawler and reluctant flyer" who finds it as hard as the aphids to believe in my own power of flight. My atrophied wings are more likely than not pressed tightly to my body, their hardened outer cover trying more to shield me from perceived harm than to help me soar to the heavens that are my inheritance.

This last chapter, the end of your own Jubilee Year, is the most important. If you "get" anything from this journey you have set out on this past year, get this: you have wings and they were meant to be used. They are to take you beyond your wildest dreams to the center of the Godself, where you will understand with all your being that you are a pure and perfect expression of God/dess.

So go through the final pre-flight check, pull up your ailerons and taxi to the end of the runway. You have been cleared for takeoff. The last leg of your journey is about to begin!

WEEK ONE

Wing buds

We are destined to fly

Gifts upon the shore
May 5, 1996

It's almost time to leave the coast. I came here a week ago, to begin to heal after I lost my job. But now I'm ready to pack up the treasures I've collected as I've strolled the beach, the ones spread out across the kitchen table. There are a few small shells, none still intact, looking strangely like white angel wings; one lone moonstone; a strangely compelling piece of driftwood slightly larger than the palm of my hand, its surface still wet from the ocean and covered with sand.

I was drawn to each of these because they held some meaning for me. The moonstone, for instance, reminds me of when I was a young child, and my father and I would go beachcombing and tidepooling. I can still feel the wind on my face, the brightly colored bandanna around my neck, the T-shirt, pedal pushers, and low-cut tennis shoes squishy with salt water. I would delight in the moonstones, taking them home and storing them in my small pirate treasure chest. Somehow I lost track of this treasure chest after I grew up, but to this day I still remember the shape, size, color and feel of my favorite stones.

It's odd that I found only one moonstone today. Usually I find many. It makes me think of the black and white stones that determined the fate of a citizen on trial in ancient Rome. Their judges would file by a box, one by one, and put in either a black or white stone. A preponderance of black stones signaled exile — of white, innocence. I have been exiled, but the stone I hold is a solitary gem, translucent, milky white, letting the sun's rays through it while showing its own unique inner beauty. And I know I'm not alone, not really in exile, not disconnected from the Source. No earthly power can do that to me.

The shells are another sign. They look like angel wings, reminding me I am truly meant to fly. And the piece of driftwood has a strangely comforting shape, evocative of something that eludes definition. I take it in hand, turn it around, eye it from every angle. Then it hits me. It is my goddess self, those strange "buds", one on each side, on the verge of becoming rudimentary wings. She will go on my altar to remind me that it is my destiny to fly.

Icarus
June 29, 1996

I see the figure every day on my way to the Cosmos Cafe — a bright orange, yellow and red paper maché form of the classical Greek figure, Icarus, falling from heaven, hung outside the art center. As the story goes, his father, Daedalus, black-smith to the gods, fashioned himself wings held together by wax so he could fly. Icarus insisted on his own pair of wings but, heedless of his father's warnings, he flew too close to the sun, melting his wings and plunging to his death.

The stories of the ancient Greeks have come down to us through the centuries, influencing our literature, our art, but more deeply, how we see our human existence. The message from the Icarus story is crystal clear, even after two millenia. We cannot be too proud, too "full of ourselves," or there will be a divine accounting. This is doubly reinforced by our Judaeo-Christian tradition which, sadly, has focused on sin and weakness and the need for a savior outside of ourselves.

But I am no longer captive to my theological past. How unlike this limited and ultimately damning vision of hell is that of a parable preached by Sultan Walad, son of the great 13th-century Persian mystic, Rumi[1]. He claimed that a human being must be born twice, once from the mother, and once again from one's own body and her own existence. The body is like an egg, and the essence of humans must become birds in that egg through the warmth of love. When that happens we can escape from our bodies and fly to the eternal world of the soul beyond time and space.

On the whole, I'd have to say it is a greater sin to refuse to accept or acknowledge my own wings than to take a chance on flying too high.

EXERCISE

• JOURNAL

There is a story told of a man who found an eagle egg and placed it under one of his hens to hatch. She grew up with her much smaller nestmates, all the while thinking she was a chicken, scratching for food and clucking and cackling. One day, when she was very old, she looked into the sky and saw a magnificent bird flying. When she asked what it was, her sister replied, "That's an eagle, the king of the birds, not like one of us." Believing her, she ended her life as a chicken — for that was what she thought she was. What feelings and thoughts does this parable bring up in you?

• INNER WORK

In prayer or meditation, picture yourself sitting under the warm noonday sun. Feel the air on your face, caressing you. Feel your shoulders starting to itch, then pushing up and out until you have wings, folded against your side. Then feel them lifting, lifting toward the sky. Soon you are running, then your feet lift from the ground and the air holds you up as you soar above the trees. Soon you are riding the thermals, wings held out to their fullest span, gazing down at the lakes and mountains, the farms and villages. Fly until you tire, then alight on the ground to return to your human form, knowing now that you truly have wings when you need to use them.

• EXERCISE

Look into a mirror and say, over and over again, "I am _____ and I have wings. I was meant to fly." Do this until it no longer feels strange.

• YEAR OF JUBILEE COLLAGE

Find/draw a picture of wings or a bird to put on your collage.

NOTES

WEEK TWO

First flight

We need to try out our wings

I was Cleopatra in another incarnation
July 5, 1996

Have you ever wondered how people who believe in reincarnation and who claim to actually have memories of their previous lives always seem to have been famous historical figures like Cleopatra, Napoleon, George Washington, Joan of Arc? Great deeds and royal lineages roll off their tongues, and who dares challenge them? But I can see their point. Who would want to have just been George, a farm lad mucking out the stables, or a slave on a southern plantation? But maybe these psychic "wannabes" have captured a truth greater than the sometimes questionable lives they claim to have lived. Maybe they've caught a glimpse of their own glory, but it seems too frightening or seemingly out of reach in this lifetime. So they project it back into history.

Rumi[2] challenges that fear that holds us all in an impoverished world-view:

...don't be satisfied with stories, how things
Have gone with others. Unfold
Your own myth...

Start walking...
Your legs will get heavy
and tired. Then comes a moment

Of feeling the wings you've grown,
lifting.

And so...let me introduce my true self. I am Mary Heron Dyer, gardener, poet, writer, lover of life, peacemaker, healer and mystic and my wings are lifting, lifting....

God
May 26, 1996

I got up early this Sunday morning, took a walk, played in my garden, then got ready to go to the store for some bark mulch. I reached into the back of the closet for a sweatshirt, and had pulled it on before I realized there was a button on it. The button said "God." I couldn't remember when I had last worn the shirt, or where the button had come from. But I knew I didn't feel quite up to the stares I imagined the button would attract, so I took it off.

In orthodox Christian theology there is a very clear distinction between God and creation, between the eternal and temporal, between the all-pure and the "born in sin." But in Unity teaching the separation doesn't exist. We are spiritual beings having a physical experience; we are one with the Godself, worthy, pure, creative, spiritual beings. It has been hard for me to switch, symbolized by my hesitation to put on the sweatshirt.

Later in the morning I did something I hadn't done in some time — I went to a Catholic mass. A woman friend was preaching, and I wanted to hear her. It was an intriguing and challenging dance, being back at a mass. I found that some prayers I could still say; others sounded false to me and I kept my silence.

After the consecration of the Eucharist, the rest of the congregation knelt as I remained sitting, listening to them all proclaim, in preparation to receive what they believed to be the body of Christ in the form of bread, "Lord, I am not worthy to receive you, but only say the word and I shall be healed."

And I knew, then, that I was on the other side. I had walked through a door and there was no turning back. I know that I am already part of the Godself, as were all of those kneeling around me. As part of this Godself, I am and always have been worthy. No, I do not claim to be all of God, any more than a cell of the body is the whole body. But I am this particular part of God/dess now in the universe, loving, laughing, crying, living out my Godself here and now.

So next time I wear that sweatshirt I think I'll put the "God" button back on it. Because I am, pure and simple, Godself expressing. And so are you.

EXERCISE

• JOURNAL

Write about your own experience/personal history of sin, salvation and redemption. Have you ever or do you now feel the need to be "saved?" Do you still define yourself as a "sinner?" What kind of feelings come up when you think of yourself as a part of the Godself expressing?

• INNER WORK

In prayer or meditation, picture yourself in a beautiful place, restful and peaceful. Gradually feel yourself becoming more and more transparent until you are pure light, glowing, warm, harmonious and whole. Stay there awhile, experiencing your goodness, your grace, your inherent worth and beauty.

• EXERCISE

Put the word "God" or "Goddess" on your mirror. Stare into it, seeing your face over the sign. What does it feel like? Keep it up until it feels natural.

• YEAR OF JUBILEE COLLAGE

Write out the word "God," "Goddess" or whatever word you use for higher power. Find a picture of yourself or a small mirror, mount it next to the word and place them on your collage.

NOTES

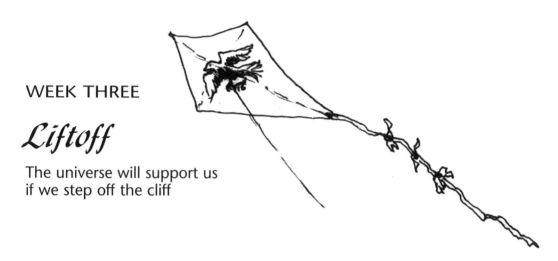

WEEK THREE

Liftoff

The universe will support us
if we step off the cliff

What is the meaning of life?

January 23, 1997

I went to hospice training last night, after a long day at school. The subject was communication, but I sneaked a peek at next week's reading assignment — spirituality. As I leafed through the section, I ran across a beautiful tale called "The Meaning of Life," an excerpt from Robert Fulghum's book, *It Was on Fire When I Lay Down on It*[3]. Here he tells the story of a small Cretan village during World War II, decimated by Nazi executions after the partisans attacked them when they invaded Crete. One man, Alexander Papaderos, then a small boy, survived to grow up to make the reconciliation of the Greeks and the Germans his life's work. To this end he built an institute among the graveyards of those killed during the war.

One day, Fulghum, at the end of a two-week conference, asked him one final question: "What is the meaning of life?"

After the anticipated laughter came the unanticipated response: "I will answer your question."

With that Papaderos took his wallet out of his hip pocket, fished into a leather billfold and brought out a very round mirror, the size of a quarter. He recounted the story of that small fragment by saying he had found it as a young boy, the largest piece of metal and glass left of a German motorcycle that had been wrecked on that small war-torn island.

Initially, with a small boy's enthusiasm, he had tried to find all the pieces to fit them together, but it was not possible. So he kept the largest one, polishing it on a stone over and over again until it shone brightly. It became a favorite toy for the boy, who learned to use this little bit of mirror to reflect light into more and more inaccessible places as his skill grew.

He kept the mirror as he grew into a man, taking it out from time to time to play his childhood game. But the toy of his boyhood became a beacon leading him into the light of full maturity. He learned that this small piece of light was really a way to understand his task as an adult, to shine light into all the dark places of life, into all the hatred and fear, which could only thrive in darkness.

He concluded,

"I am a fragment of a mirror whose whole design and shape I do not know. Nevertheless, with what I have I can reflect light into the dark places of this world — into the black places in the hearts of men — and change some things in some people. Perhaps others may see and do likewise. This is what I am about. This is the meaning of my life."

And with that Fulghum ends,

"he took his small mirror and, holding it carefully, caught the bright rays of the daylight streaming through the window and reflected them onto my face and onto my hands folded on the desk...in the wallet of my mind I carry a small round mirror still. Are there any questions?"

"We're remembering, we're awakening..."
April 6, 1997

A week of fatigue and resistance, of being overwhelmed by my own ambitions. I started a class on tree-trimming—during the first class we learned how to coil ropes, loop them over tree limbs, get into harnesses, tie ourselves safely into the line (two half-hitches, a figure eight, another knot around the other half of the rope, then another figure eight to finish it off). I both loved it and was terrified, but it totally did me in. With a mixture of regret and relief, I dropped the class.

Spring is playing cat and mouse. A few warm moments, then a gust of cold air makes me turn up my collar and hunker down into my jacket.

My business is picking up. I have four active clients right now (one biweekly maintenance, one weekly maintenance/landscaping, one lawn removal including replanting and path construction, and one landscaping). In three weeks I'll sit down to plan the implementation of an irrigation system for a fifth, and I received two unsolicited referrals over the weekend. My cup runneth over!

Meanwhile the buds are breaking out in stunning pinks and whites, fuchsias, purples, reds, lavenders, green. Somehow the seemingly dead wood remembered its promise over winter and renewed its vows to life in every blossom, every blade of grass.

In church today we had a beautiful meditation hymn, whose first verse goes:

We're remembering,
We're awakening,
We create love.[4]

It helped me understand and accept the process of my own forgetting and remembering, my own going to sleep and awakening, the resistance I feel to my own joy. My own success, my own Godself, is much more powerful than the winter's last weakening hold on spring.

Those without visible means of support...
November 11, 1996

Yesterday was a fluke day for this time of year at the coast — sunny, mild and very warm. We walked on the beach at low tide, picking up isolated pebbles left by the receding waters, playing tag with the waves and watching the seagulls soar.

As I observed their crisp white outlines against the piercingly blue cloudless sky, I saw the seagulls floating, swooping, soaring, not a feather ruffled, not even a wing moving. Without visible means of support, suspended in "thin" air, they trust in its invisible yet constant support so strong they never even think to doubt it.

And I envied them. They were born knowing what I am still struggling to learn — absolute, unwavering faith that the universal presence that holds the seagull unfailing in the piercing blue sky will hold me as well. For those without visible means of support...fly!

EXERCISE

• JOURNAL

"Keep what is worth keeping and with a breath of kindness blow the rest away." You are now nearing the end of your Year of Jubilee. You are about to "fly." What do you still need to let go of that is weighing you down?

• INNER WORK

In prayer or meditation, imagine yourself in the audience with Robert Fulghum on that tiny Cretan island. If he asked you the question, "What is the meaning of life?" what would you respond?

• EXERCISE

Look at what you wrote for the exercise in Chapter I, Week 2, "Johari's Window." What can you now add or change in the sections "What you know about yourself" and "What everyone knows about you" boxes?

• YEAR OF JUBILEE COLLAGE

Underneath the wings, feather or bird picture from last week, write your own name.

WEEK FOUR

Godself achieved

We are all part of the Godself expressing

"All manner of thing shall be well"
December 24, 1996

Up early to grade papers and continue entering my journal onto the computer. Midmorning I took a break to look at *Unity Magazine*. Then I had an idea — I decided to submit several of my journal entries to the editor, with the suggestion that he consider a monthly column. Stranger things have happened! That took me until early afternoon, when I braved the pre-Christmas lines at the post office to mail my journal priority mail to Unity Village in Missouri.

Next, a long talk on the phone with Vilik, who continues to have adventures in her month in Santa Cruz.

Church was awesome, a musical, meditative, candlelight service. At the end we each held a candle as we circled the room, filling the church with light — over 120 people. It was miraculous to see all the candlelit, Christ-filled faces.

Then to a party, home for another long phone talk with my partner, then… into the silence. Everything is ready for tomorrow, presents wrapped. Into the silence…into the silence.

Tonight people all over the world celebrate the coming of The Word into this world, The Word of peace which passes all understanding, that opens our eyes to wonder and stills our tongues, as T. S. Eliot so eloquently expresses in his poem "Burnt Norton", part of *The Four Quartets*[5]:

Words move, music moves
Only in time; but that which
Is only living
Can only die. Words, after speech, reach
Into the silence. Only by the form, the pattern,
Can words or music reach
The stillness.

And in this stillness, this place beyond words, I know that through this birthday of God-become-flesh I celebrate my own birth. God's journey through Jesus is a forerunner of my own.

Easter Sunday
March 29, 1997

It's almost midnight. I had a full day — landscaping, a trip to Eugene to visit with my elder daughter, complete with preparing her garden and seeing "Secrets and Lies," grading, watching ice skating, playing with Hilda, my pet hedgehog (named after the famous medieval English abbess, poet, musician, writer, theologian, Hildegard of Bingen), and Flame, our Italian greyhound. But now it's very quiet. Everyone has gone home, the whole house is quiet and I sit at my kitchen table pondering the mystery that is Easter.

I played the "Alleluia" tape all the way back from Eugene, driving into the growing darkness, feeling a peace and stillness descend on me, knowing that all over the world Christians are preparing to celebrate Easter.

A few years ago I would have done these past few days to the hilt — Holy Thursday liturgy followed by a Passover meal, a Good Friday service with the stations of the cross, and, finally, after the waiting and the darkness, driving to a church for midnight mass, where the candles lit from the Pascal candle would glimmer as each newly lit taper added its soft glow to the expectant and hushed congregation.

But tonight I'm not so much waiting for the annual enactment of Christ's resurrection, but silently, prayerfully, acknowledging that this drama of death and rebirth, of seeing the Christ spirit conquer death, is as much about me as Jesus. It has to be. My spirit, my life force, has over and over again encountered death and each time, just like the spring, it has triumphed over death.

In the silence, in the darkness, the Christ spirit is resurrected from the dead — in this place, at this time, in me. Alleluia!

EXERCISE

• JOURNAL

T. S. Eliot, in the last lines of his famous "Little Gidding,"[6] the last of the *Four Quartets*, sums up the whole poem with these lines, "And all shall be well and/All manner of thing shall be well ...." What do you think about, vision for, the sum total of your own life?

• INNER WORK

There is a story told of a doll made of salt who wandered her whole life in quest of who she was. One day, after many years of wandering, she saw the ocean in the distant horizon and walked toward it. After she came to the shore she walked slowly into the water, dissolving at every step until she was part of the ocean. In prayer or meditation, take the journey of that salt doll.

• EXERCISE

Go to a park, mall, library, or store. Sit someplace quietly, and as each person passes by, see yourself in them and silently bless them.

• YEAR OF JUBILEE COLLAGE

Find/draw something that represents for you your own Godself.

CHAPTER TWELVE ENDNOTES

1. Harvey, Andrew. *The Way of Passion: A Celebration of Rumi*. Frog Limited: Berkeley, 1994.

2. Rumi. *These Branching Moments*. Translated by Coleman Barks. Copper Beech Press: Providence, RI: Brown University, 1988.

3. Fulghum, Robert. *It Was On Fire When I Lay Down On It*. New York: Random House, 1989.

4. Written by Kathy Zavada.

5. Eliot, T. S. "Burnt Norton." *The Four Quartets*. Harcourt Brace & Company: NY, 1971.

6. Eliot, T. S. "Little Gidding." *The Four Quartets*. Harcourt Brace & Company: NY, 1971.

Afterword

*I*t's a beautiful, archetypal summer day. We are at the river again, Vilik and I. Vilik is sitting, as usual, in her favorite spot, in full afternoon sun, her feet dangling in a rivulet as the cold water swirls by on its insistent rush to the sea. Flame, our "equal-opportunity," twelve-pound Italian greyhound, keeps walking gingerly on the rounded river stones back and forth between a sunny spot on a rock by Vilik and my chair, set up under an overhang with lots of shade, where she finds a softer and cooler resting place on my lap.

It's been almost 16 months since my own Year of Jubilee officially ended and my life, just like the river's, has flowed on. I still do landscaping part-time and still work occasionally at a retail nursery. But recently I found myself again wanting to use my "people" skills professionally. And during these past months "off", as I volunteered in a hospice program and as a grief group leader, I discovered the population I want to work with.

Just a few weeks ago I began a half-time job as volunteer coordinator at a large and progressive facility offering living alternatives for elders. It's a different "feel" than crisis work, going home without either a beeper on my hip or a weight on my heart. And I love the commitment to humanize the environment for both staff and residents. Animals, including birds in an aviary and bunny babies, abound.... I'm as likely to meet a pooch in the hall as a person. I'm slowly building up my professional wardrobe, trying to make the switch from knee-pads to knee-highs as gracefully as possible.

I live just next door to the "thunder mug" apartment, in a house I purchased last spring. I walked by that "for sale" sign for months before the light bulb lit up and I realized "my" house was right there, a stone's throw from my window. I have a large, fenced backyard I'm slowly landscaping, my living room has a fireplace, and the extra bedroom is now my office and the new home of Dandelion Seed Press, begun the winter of last year. Outside the office window I've planted a redbud; in front of the living room window, a hawthorne. They're just saplings right now, but next spring the redbud will have purple flowers and the hawthorne's red blossoms will turn to red berries that will brighten my view into the winter.

I hope the time we've spent together through this book has delighted you, challenged you, and given you solace on your own journey toward the abundant ocean of life that has always been your inheritance. Flowing, tumbling at times, over the boulders in your own life, you were always, and always are, going towards your soul's destination. And your courage as, after yet another of those tumbles, you surrender once again to the inevitable journey, is a constant source of hope to me.

Blessings,

Mary Heron Dyer
August 19, 1998
Cascadia State Park
Oregon

Bibliography

Bach, Richard. *Illusions: The Adventures of a Reluctant Messiah*. NY: Delacorte Press, 1977.

Brox, Jane. *Here and Nowhere Else*. Boston: Beacon Press, 1995.

Catton, Bruce, adapted from "The Joy Above the Stars, the Terror Below the Ice," in *Waiting for the Morning Train*. Doubleday and Co: NY, 1972.

Cayce, Edgar. *You'll See it When You Believe It*. William Morrow Company Inc: NY, 1989.

Chopra, Deepak. *The Seven Spiritual Laws of Success: A Practical Guide to the Fulfillment of Your Dreams*. Amber-Allen Publishing Company: San Rafael, CA, 1994.

Daly, Mary. *Beyond God the Father: Toward a Philosophy of Women's Liberation*. Boston: Beacon Press, 1973.

Dinesen, Isak. "The Monkey," from *Seven Gothic Tales*. NY: Vintage Books, 1972.

Douglas, David. *The Oregon Journals of David Douglas, of his Travels and Adventures among the Traders and Indians in the Columbia, Willamette and Snake River Regions During the Years 1825, 1826 and 1927,* (Publisher, publication date unknown).

Dyer, Wayne. *You'll See It When You Believe It: The Way to Your Personal Transformation*. William Morrow and Co. Inc: NY, 1989.

Eliot, T.S. Excerpt from "The Love Song of J. Alfred Prufrock," from *Collected Poems 1909-1935*. Harcourt, Brace and World, Inc.: NY, 1936.

Eliot, T. S. Excerpt from "Burnt Norton," from *The Four Quartets*. Harcourt Brace & Company: NY, 1971.

Fulghum, Robert. *It Was On Fire When I Lay Down On It*. NY: Random House, 1989.

Gilligan, Carol. *In a Different Voice: Psychological Theory and Women's Development*. Cambridge: Harvard University Press, 1982.

Harvey, Andrew. *The Way of Passion: A Celebration of Rumi*. Frog Limited: Berkeley, 1994.

Heinrich, Bernd. *A Year in the Maine Wood*. Addison-Wesley Publication Co.: Reading, MA, 1994.

Hein, Piet. *Grooks*. Doubleday and Co.: NY, 1966.

Holmes, Oliver Wendell."The Chambered Nautilus," from *The Complete Poems of Oliver Wendell Holmes*. Houghton-Mifflin Co.: NY, 1927.

The Jerusalem Bible. NY: Doubleday & Company, Inc., 1966.

Kingsolver, Barbara. *The Bean Trees*. Harper and Row: NY, 1988.

Lindbergh, Anne Morrow. *Gift from the Sea*. NY: Random House, Inc., 1955.

Martin, Wendy. *An American Triptych: Anne Bradshaw, Emily Dickenson, Adrienne Rich*. Chapel Hill: University of North Carolina Press, 1986.

Millay, Edna St. Vincent. "Afternoon on a Hill," from *Collected Poems*. Harper and Row Publishers: NY, 1956.

Myss, Carolyn. *Anatomy of the Spirit: The Seven Stages of Power and Healing*. Harmony Books: NY, 1966.

Oliver, Mary. "The Deer," from *New and Selected Poems*. Beacon Press: Boston, 1992.

Orman, Suze. *The 9 Steps to Financial Freedom*. NY: Crown Publishers, 1997.

Piercy, Marge. *Circles in the Water: Selected Poems of Marge Piercy*. Alfred Knopf: NY, 1983.

Piercy, Marge. "For Strong Women," from *The Moon is Always Female*. Alfred Knopf, Inc: NY, 1980.

Rich, Adrienne. "What is Possible," from *A Wild Patience Has Taken Me This Far: Poems 1978-1981*. W.W. Norton & Co.: NY, 1981.

Rosen, Kim. "In Impossible Darkness." *Naked Waters*, CD and cassette on EarthSea Records ©1998.

Rumi, *These Branching Moments*. Translated by Coleman Barks. Copper Beech Press, NY, 1988

Salzberg, Susan. *Loving-Kindness: The Revolutionary Art of Happiness*. Shambhala: Boston, 1995.

Stevenson, Jody. *Soul Purpose: Rediscover Your Creative Genius and Become the Champion of Your Life*. Portland, OR: Source Communications & Publishing: 1995.

Tao te Ching by Lao Tzu, A New English Version, with Foreword and Notes by Stephen Mitchell. Harper and Row, Publishers: NY, 1988.

Tolkein, J.R.R. *The Hobbit* (revised edition). Ballantine Books: NY, 1966.

Walsch, Neale Donald. *Conversations With God: An Uncommon Dialogue*. G.P. Putnam and Sons: NY, 1996.

Yeats, William Butler. "The Lake Isle of Innisfree." From *Collected Poems*. NY: Macmillan, 1956.

ABOUT THE AUTHOR

Mary Heron Dyer fell into her Year of Jubilee the hard way — by getting fired — from her job as coordinator of volunteers at a domestic violence agency.

It was a challenging loss. She was already in midlife. And her work, combining counseling skills with women's issues, had become her identity as well as her newly found financial security.

During her 20-year marriage the sometimes threadbare but at least consistent cushion of her husband's income had allowed her, while also mothering three children, to pursue masters' degrees in English literature and scripture and theology. Catholic parish ministry followed, including teaching, counseling and organizing; she also became a much published theological writer.

When, for her own growth, she left her two most important support systems, her marriage and the Catholic church, a new journey began. With no easily marketable skills she tried her hand at everything from salmon tagger to bed and breakfast host, nurse's aide to tutor, dishwasher to carpenter, while along the way she discovered and became involved in women's issues. Her challenges and adventures were expressed as fiction in a women's murder mystery, *A Ship in the Harbor*.

Finally deciding on a counseling career to develop the skills and interests begun in ministry, she entered the graduate counseling program at Oregon State University; after graduation she went on to work at the domestic violence agency previously mentioned. Meanwhile her long spiritual search was ending as she discovered *New Thought* — a liberating and empowering vision of people as direct expressions of God/Goddess/All That Is — in the form of Unity church.

For a time, as on one hand she attended a church that spoke of inner power and on the other worked in a system that sometimes reinforced an image of women as victims, the worlds of new thought and women's issues seemed to collide. Her firing from the agency became ultimately a gift, a gift of time during which she was able to grapple with and finally encompass all the "truths" of her life, to see the problems women face realistically while at the same time holding them in the context of ultimate possibility. *Year of Jubilee* is the result.

Mary currently lives in Corvallis, Oregon, with her woman partner, Vilik, their dog, Flame, and Mary's hedgehog, Hildegard. She's a self-employed landscaper and one-woman publishing company, works part-time as coordinator of volunteers at a facility for elders and also at a plant nursery, and volunteers at hospice and as a facilitator for a grief group. She's served on the board of Unity of Corvallis, is studying to be a licensed Unity teacher and occasionally gives the Sunday talk. She especially enjoys her own garden and her three grown children.

OPPORTUNITIES FOR CHURCHES AND GROUPS

In addition to being a gardener and writer, Mary Heron Dyer is a counselor and public speaker. She is available to give the message at church services and to speak before groups, formally or informally. She also leads *Year of Jubilee* workshops and can create an exciting and thought-provoking weekend experience for interested churches.

Mary's style is informal, with liberal use of humor, yet always informed by her theological background, enlightened by her understanding of the universe as supportive and loving, and enlivened by her personal experience.

Although *Year of Jubilee* was written with women in mind, Mary's talks reflect issues and truths common to everyone. Her workshops can be open to all or focused on women.

If your church or group would like to explore the powerful option of taking the ideas of *Year of Jubilee* beyond individual experience, Mary Heron Dyer can be reached c/o Dandelion Seed Press, 946 NW Circle Blvd. #282, Corvallis, OR 97330; telephone (541) 753-2819.

Dandelion Seed
P R E S S

It is children who see the beauty of the ubiquitous dandelion, who pick its homely little yellow flowers and blow with gusto its fuzzy-headed seed pods into the wind. The mission of Dandelion Seed Press is to spread that childlike delight, that sense of divine inheritance and unabashed expression of radiant aliveness, as far and wide as the dandelion itself.

ORDER FORM

☎ **TELEPHONE ORDERS**
Call (541) 753-2819
Have your VISA or MasterCard ready.

✐ **ON-LINE ORDERS**
Email this information to dandelionseed@proaxis.com

✉ **POSTAL ORDERS**
Dandelion Seed Press, 946 NW Circle Blvd. #282, Corvallis, OR 97330

PLEASE SEND _____ **COPIES OF** *Year of Jubilee* (ISBN 0-9666448-7-5).

(at retail price of $18.95 each) $ _____

Discounts:
    1-3   books .No discount
    4-6   books . . . . .20% off
    7-10   books . . . . .30% off
    10 +   books . . . . .40% off

SHIPPING
$4.00 for the first book and $2.00 each for each
additional book. (Shipped USPO Fourth Class) $ _____

TOTAL COST $ _____

PAYMENT
    ☐ Check   ☐ Credit card: ☐ VISA   ☐ MasterCard

    Card number _____   Exp. date ____ / _____

    Name on card _____

Company name _____

Name _____

Address _____

City_____ State_____ Zip _____ – _____

ORDER FORM

☎ **TELEPHONE ORDERS**
Call (541) 753-2819
Have your VISA or MasterCard ready.

✐ **ON-LINE ORDERS**
Email this information to dandelionseed@proaxis.com

✉ **POSTAL ORDERS**
Dandelion Seed Press, 946 NW Circle Blvd. #282, Corvallis, OR 97330

PLEASE SEND _____ COPIES OF *Year of Jubilee* (ISBN 0-9666448-7-5).
   (at retail price of $18.95 each) $ _____

   Discounts:
        1-3   books . . . . .No discount
        4-6   books . . . . .20% off
        7-10   books . . . . .30% off
        10 +   books . . . . .40% off

SHIPPING
   $4.00 for the first book and $2.00 each for each
   additional book. (Shipped USPO Fourth Class) $ _____

TOTAL COST $ _____

PAYMENT
        ☐ Check   ☐ Credit card: ☐ VISA   ☐ MasterCard

   Card number _____ Exp. date ____ / _____

   Name on card _____

Company name _____

Name _____

Address _____

City_____ State_____ Zip _____